The Literary Connection

VOLUME I

Editors:

Cheryl Antao-Xavier

Nina Munteanu

Merridy Cox Bradley

Saima S. Hussain

An IOWI Anthology

THE LITERARY CONNECTION
VOLUME I

Publisher: In Our Words Inc.
www.inourwords.ca
inourwords@bell.net

Book design: Shirley Aguinaldo

Cover design: Steve Czajka - flickr.com/photos/steveczajka

Library and Archives Canada Cataloguing in Publication

The literary connection / editors: Cheryl Antao-Xavier,
Nina Munteanu, Merridy Cox Bradley, Saima S. Hussain.

"An IOWI anthology"--Title page, volume 1.
ISBN 978-1-926926-45-2 (v. 1 : pbk.)

1. Canadian literature (English)--21st century.
I. Munteanu, Nina, editor II. Antao-Xavier, Cheryl, 1957-, editor
III. Hussain, Saima S., editor IV. Cox Bradley, Merridy, editor

PS8251.1.L58 2014 C810.8'006 C2014-905856-X

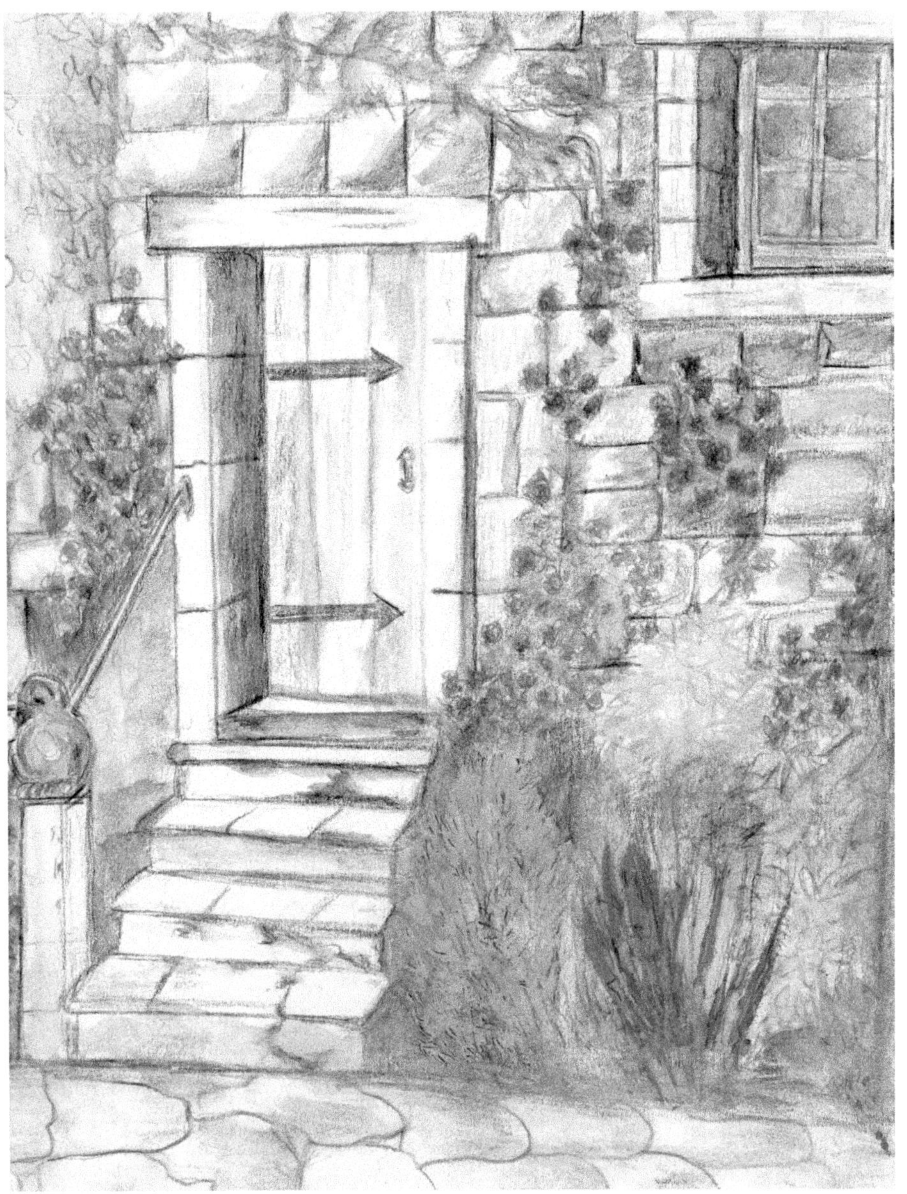

'Front Door' by Carmela Zita-Kapeleris

CONTENTS

IMAGES

(in order of appearance)

WELCOME TO THE ANTHOLOGY:
The Literary Connection
VOLUME I

The twenty literary works provided within the covers of this Canadian anthology represent a vivid diversity of writing style, genre, experience, heritage and place. From allegory to anecdote, these tales span from comedic to tragic, as authors and poets of all ages examine themes that touch our hearts and give us pause. Themes of inspiration and triumph, of life's ironies, both tragic and hilarious. Themes of love and loss and sharing. Themes of wonder for our natural environment. This collection explores our Canadian sense of identity and place, from the eyes of an aging immigrant to the touch of a native youth. From wise to irreverent, authors share life-changes and milestones over their many years of living, loving and sharing. And in all cases, using the vernacular of unique Canadian expression and humour.

This chaotic soup of expression embraces complexity, multiplicity and even paradox. What better way to begin a Canadian anthology series than by celebrating the multiverse of what Canada is: *Do I contradict myself? Very well, then I contradict myself, I am large, I contain multitudes* (Walt Whitman).

Enjoy these twenty very different stories and poems. They will make you dream, reflect, wonder and smile. They will certainly make you laugh. Now, isn't that Canadian?

—*The Editors*

Peta-Gaye Nash

SERIOUS POETRY

Jean McDonald was coming back from a poetry group in Brampton that met bi-monthly. It was a little way from her home in West Mississauga but she liked the people in the group. It wasn't just a bunch of artsy fartsies but there were actually people from other countries in South Asia, Asia and the Middle East. It made for an interesting group. Their poetry was all about war and death and rebirth and integration. It made Jean's eyes water to hear these tragedies which floated out of lips that spoke English with thick accents. Their poetry sounded authentic as if they knew everything there was to know about human suffering.

In contrast, her poetry was light and fluffy. She found that before she read, she always apologized for her poetry's lightness but she loved it when she made people laugh. The intent of her poetry, she told people, was to make them feel good. Yet still, she apologized for it. She sometimes thought from the looks on people's faces that they didn't think her poetry was serious enough, that it wasn't the real deal. They smiled at her indulgently as she read, as if they were smiling down at a child and they laughed politely. Jean couldn't help it though. It was what came out of her: sunny brightness like the sunshine that poured through her kitchen windows where she sat and wrote every day. Her kitchen was bright, even during the cold dark winter months because of the large windows, the skylight and the fact that the kitchen faced east.

The poetry group, thought Jean as she drove, made writing worthwhile. There were so many people who didn't appreciate the time it took to construct a poem or the searing beauty of it. It made her want to sing. Just that night a man wrote of hiding under a mahogany table, terrified, while war planes flew overhead. She lived that man's nightmare for five minutes. She who had lived in Canada all her life and had never known war, knew what it felt like to hear the rat-a-tat-tat of machine guns and breathe the acrid smoke from burning houses and hear women wailing in fear and grief.

It was too bad that Brampton was so far. When she was a child it had been all farmland. As far as she knew, only farmers lived out there in brick houses spaced miles apart from each other. Now the highway stretched all the way out and she could get to Brampton quickly. It was a pain in the neck during the winter, although, driving anywhere was hard during winter's snowstorms and icy roads. But she still made the effort to go to the poetry group.

Now it was late fall and the evenings were shorter. It was nine when Jean was saying her drawn out goodbyes, nine-thirty when she got into her little electric blue Mazda 3 and drove away.

She was still thinking about the man who grew up in Pakistan and who had hidden under the mahogany table when she realized she missed the road that would take her to highway 427. The roads were all new and her GPS, which she'd meant to update for ages, was giving the wrong directions. Jean, who laughingly told people she got lost on the way home from the supermarket, got disoriented and turned down another road. The road was badly lit and empty. She wondered if she should do a quick U-turn to get back on track. She decided against it and turned down another road meaning to circle back. She looked right, then she looked left to make sure no other car was coming. Then she stepped on the gas and turned right while still looking left and hit something hard. At first she didn't know what had happened but the impact was so great that she automatically stomped on the brakes.

She looked back. It was a man, no a boy, and he had come out of nowhere. Where on earth did he come from? The boy lay face down, sprawled on the road. From what she could see, he was wearing all black—jacket, pants, even his sneakers were black.

"Are you alright?" she called out, with her head out the window. She knew she should call 911 but something stopped her. "Are you alright, I'm so sorry, you there?"

There was no answer. If she got out of the car, someone might attack her. It might be a ruse. The crime in Brampton was bad what with all the recent immigration. She should sit in her car and call 911. There was no one around. It was dark. She could wait for another car but the road was deserted. She should simply call 911. Jean put the phone in her purse, looked around, looked at the boy still lying there and drove off.

It was so out of character.

Jean drove home praying that the boy lived. If he lived, she would be okay. If he died, she would go to jail, lose her license or her job. Maybe even her husband John of forty years might leave her. He was always saying she drove carelessly and she'd never gotten a speeding ticket yet he had. Jean didn't think she could survive jail. What had just happened? It was unreal. She heard things like this on the news about other people who left the scene of an accident; wicked, cruel people who had no place in civilized society.

Back at home, John asked how her poetry group went. He usually never asked how it went. "Fine," she mumbled. She should confide in him. He would fix it. He always fixed everything. Sure, he would ask her how she could've done such a heinous thing as leaving but after he'd ranted a bit, he would calm down and call the police and drive out there to make sure the boy was still alive.

"Why don't we watch a movie tonight?" he asked.

It was like he was trying to torment her. Usually he left her alone after her poetry group.

"Not tonight. I don't feel well."

"What's the matter?" He looked concerned.

Jean thought: If this goes to court, he'll remember I was acting funny. I shouldn't act funny. I'll watch the movie. "On second thought, a movie would be great. Just wait a bit for me. I left something in the car. I have to go get it."

"I'll get it for you?"

"No, John. I can get it myself." She went outside, through the side garage door and turned on the light. She couldn't see clearly as she inspected the car. She was glad John couldn't see her from inside the house because the garage was detached. It was too dim to see anything because he hadn't fixed the outside lights. She looked around wildly for a cloth. Nowadays detectives could detect blood from a murder scene even if it had been wiped away with bleach. She found a bag of old clothes she'd meant to give away, opened the bag and wiped the front of the car. It would have to do for now. Tomorrow she'd take the car to an automatic car wash and then she'd rewash it again at home.

It was agony watching a comedy, *Something About Mary*, (which she had seen before and loved) when all she could think of was the boy lying there dressed in black. He had stepped out in front of her car. Didn't he see her? Silly boy! Teenagers were all like that. They walked as if they owned the road. She saw them jaywalking all the time, on their phones, listening to their earphones with not a thought for the traffic around them. Maybe he wasn't a boy. Maybe he was a short skinny man who had children. Oh heavens, help me, she prayed. Let him live.

"John must think it's odd that I keep watching the news," thought Jean. It was like she was obsessed, remote control in hand, eyes glued, neck arched, staring at the TV in their bedroom that was mounted slightly too high. She feigned the flu so she could stay in bed. He popped in every hour or so to check on her to see if she wanted to eat or if she was feeling better.

Then there it was. The six o'clock news on Global TV. A boy had been the victim of a hit-and-run. He had suffered severe head injuries and died in hospital. His name was Inderjit Singh. He attended McMaster University and was home for the weekend. There wasn't much else after that. Jean stared at the TV long after the news. As if she could bring the boy back by staring at the TV.

It was in the weekend papers. Inderjit graduated from high school last year. He'd attended an International Business and Technology Program in high school. A friend said of him: *he was a great guy, serious about his studies and a good friend. He always encouraged us to do better.* Why couldn't he have been a hoodlum, a gangster? She'd killed a valuable citizen. It always worked like that, though, didn't it?

The paper reported that no one had witnessed the accident but the police were asking the public for information. Jean knew she should go to the police station and turn herself in but it was worse now. Maybe Inderjit would've lived had she stopped or called 911; but she didn't, so he died. She took the car to the automatic car wash.

Jean's daughter Susan came over unannounced mid week. Usually Jean would've been happy but her daughter wanted to borrow her car. Jean exploded.

"Mom, what's wrong with you? Don't lend me your stupid car, then. God, Dad says you're acting all weird." Susan left.

Jean didn't go to the poetry group for three months. The members called her and asked her when she would be coming back. It was not enough to say she was busy because she'd never missed before. She told them she was looking after family matters; besides, she hadn't been writing and had nothing to share.

When Jean went back to the poetry group, she stood up a little unsteadily. Her hand was shaking. She opened her mouth, swallowed and out gushed the serious poetry Jean felt they had all been waiting for. She wrote of death and despair. She didn't do silly rhymes about housework and wanting grandchildren. She wrote of the Divine and the afterlife, of retribution and revenge. Her audience leaned slightly forward in their seats, hungering for more. They congratulated her afterwards and said things like, "Your poetry has undergone an amazing transformation." It was deep, they said; it spoke of the utter despair of the human condition. Everyone understood it. Everyone couldn't wait for more.

At the following meeting Jean wrote of waiting for death. Death with its fetid breath and maggoty mouth lurked in the shadows. It reached out to grab hold then changed its mind. Death's grip was cold and clammy; death's robe wasn't black as people thought. It was translucent 3D and one could see the evils man had done as a moving picture within the folds of Death's robe. The audience gasped with pleasure. She had written the nightmares from their dreams.

The week after that Jean wrote of escape. Escape from her anguished life where death would've been preferable. But there was no escape, certainly not in heaven, because even there, judgment is cast. Escape where there was no pain, no sickness, no ill deeds nor ill will. Escape, heaven, words, ideas created by humans to alleviate their suffering. If only they knew, there is no escape, there never was.

People were silent. The poetry was so rich. Jean's suffering was so intense, that the group members wondered if she had cancer. No one asked outright but the pity and concern were carved into their expressions.

"Did they ever find the person who hit that young boy around here?" she asked someone.

"What young boy?"

"Oh, it was several months ago. It was a hit-and-run. You didn't hear of it?"

"I vaguely remember something about that. I dunno. Why?"

"I thought it was such a pity," answered Jean. "He was so young. His name was Inderjit."

The woman she was speaking to also nodded in sympathy.

Jean wanted to travel to India. "Why?" asked her husband. She had never had that urge before. She had always wanted to travel to Scotland, Ireland or Wales. She was allowed to change her mind, wasn't she, she asked him. Well, wasn't she? He shrugged. She had gotten some strange notions in her head. Even her poetry was unrecognizable, incomprehensible. She used words and imagery he'd never heard of before. If it was a midlife crisis, it sure came late.

A publisher heard Jean reading at a local library and approached her. It was a long time since she had heard poems like that. Although poetry wasn't a big seller, she thought a book of Jean's work would do well.

The book did well. It was called *Reign of Madness*. It was dedicated to her husband John McDonald, her daughter, Susan and I.S. who died so young. Jean never told her family who I.S. was and they were puzzled by it. Universities wanted the book and for the first time, Jean and John didn't have to worry about money.

Jean wrote a second book of poems. Her publisher held the book launch at a trendy bookstore in Yorkville in Toronto. Jean chose a navy blue suit. She'd bought it at one of those ritzy Yorkville boutiques and it was well cut. She wore matching shoes and bag and her hair, once grey, was now a soft brown. It didn't make her look younger though. Her forehead was deeply lined and her mouth drew down when she wasn't smiling. She didn't smile often.

Before the book launch, Jean wanted to get coffee and something sweet from Starbucks. She hadn't eaten all day and it was now evening. She rushed out of Starbucks with the coffee in her hand. The line was long and she had to get back to the store. The public would be arriving any minute. Jean chose to cross against the lights and she didn't look where she was going. She didn't see the SUV hurtling around the corner and it knocked her flat. The coffee went flying and hit the windscreen of the SUV. Jean's head slammed into the pavement and the last thought in her head was the title of her second book, *For You, The Condemned.*

After the funeral when Susan and John were going through her things, they found an old newspaper clipping of the death of a young Sikh boy whose name was Inderjit Singh. Susan wondered if Inderjit Singh was I. S. and what did he have to do with her mother. John shrugged. He said he didn't know a thing about it.

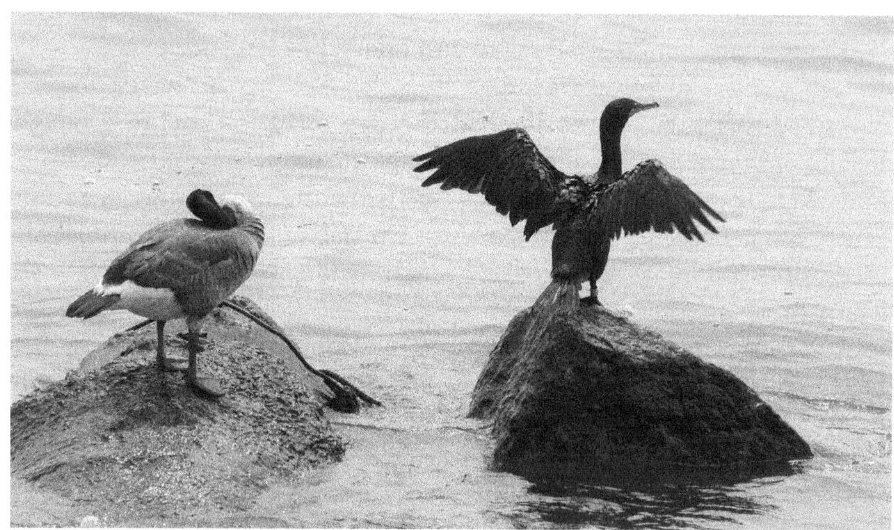

Photograph by Merridy Cox

THE PASSWORD

It was late.

"I love the silence of the night," he said to his wife. He took a long, slow pull on a freshly rolled spliff and handed it to her. She cocked her head to the side and listened.

"It's not really silent."

The wind rustled the leaves of the breadfruit tree growing tall outside their living room window and the crickets chirped their night song. She inhaled, holding the spliff delicately between long thin fingers with well-manicured nails. She felt the warmth spread from her groin to her stomach to her limbs, and she smiled.

He was sitting in a corner of the dimly lit living room where they had set up the computer, and now he peered intently at the screen. She sat on his lap, facing him, straddling him with her legs. She wanted to show him that she loved him again. She wanted to forget about the mistake that had just ended, a sordid affair with his business partner. She had gotten careless; they both had, because it was so easy. He had never questioned her.

"I'm working late again," she would tell him, night after night.

He'd smile and tell her he missed her in the evenings, watching TV all by himself.

"Don't work so hard, honey," he'd say tenderly, and her stomach would churn, sick with guilt.

But now it was over and she was relieved. The other man flirted with everyone. He began to flirt openly with her in front of her husband. It was too close. How could her husband not see it? Even his partner began to treat him differently. It was subtle, but he became condescending, as if to say 'I've got one up on you, I've got your wife.'

No, it was too close and she was glad it was over. So now she wanted to show him, wanted him to feel he was really the only one. She tried to kiss him.

"Stop. I have to check my e-mail."

She turned around and sat on his lap. "Okay. I'll check mine too."

He tap-tapped a bit, then said, "Okay, now close your eyes." He was about to type his password.

The marijuana made her giggle. "What's the big deal? I would tell you mine."

"What's yours then?"

She lied easily. "FLOWER."

He smiled and showed her his. SUPERMAN.

"Superman," she repeated and laughed a shrill, high-pitched laugh. "God, you are so trusting! You didn't even check. Obviously my password isn't 'Flower'!"

He was hurt, insulted. He looked at her and she would not stop laughing. But there was something different about her eyes. The laughter did not reach them. They were hard and cold. He shivered involuntarily.

"What is your password?" He did not smile.

She tried to kiss him but he pushed her away. He lit a cigarette; he needed something to do with his hands.

"Oh, give me a drag."

"Only if you tell me your password."

"Alright. But you won't believe me. You'll think I'm weird." She had softened again. She looked vulnerable: his beautiful wife.

"Just say it."

"V-A-G-I-N-A."

His eyes bulged wide. "Are you serious?"

"Well, I knew I'd never forget it."

"You're hilarious." He handed her the cigarette. She inhaled and laughed that high, shrill laugh. He began to hate it. It sounded so cruel, so unlike her. She could not believe she had fooled him again. How could he be so naïve?

"Got you again." She said gleefully. "Why would I have the password 'Vagina?' You are so..." She hesitated. She didn't want to call him stupid. Instead she said, "You love me, don't you?"

He was puzzled, "Yeah." He said it like a question. Shouldn't he love her?

"I mean, you trust me so much. You really love me!" she said in wonder.

She reached for his face and held it tenderly. He was not sure what he saw in her eyes. They were still hard. She kissed him, long and slow, and unbuttoned his shirt.

"Wait," he said. "What is your password?"

Peta-Gaye Nash *is the author of the short story collection* I too Hear the Drums *as well as three children's books. In 2013, she got a notable mention at the Marty Awards for emerging literary arts and her work appears in several anthologies. She is currently working on her second collection,* Told Ya, *linked short stories about life in Jamaica, and two more children's books in addition to blogging on her website. Peta-Gaye teaches English as a second language and lives in Mississauga with her husband and children.*

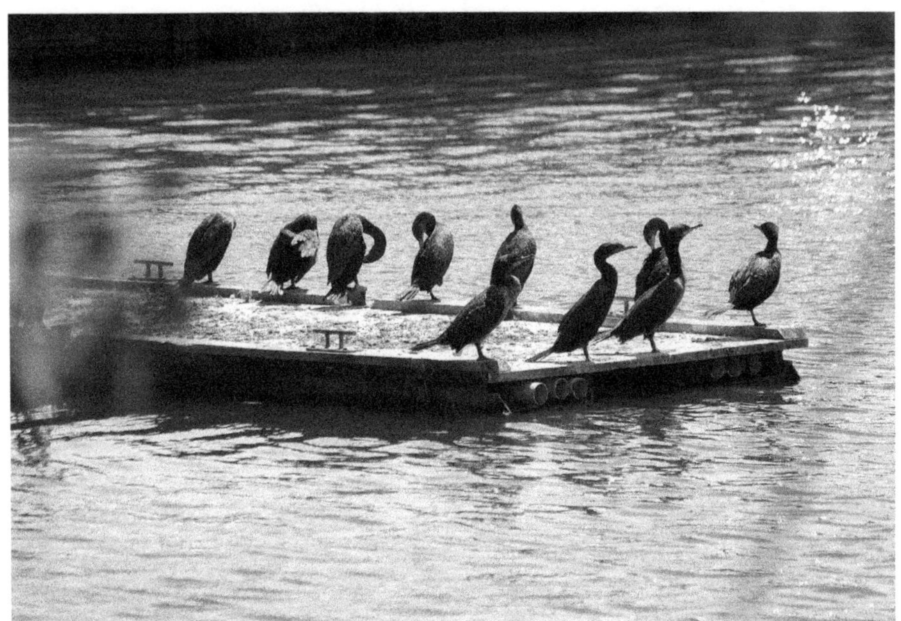

'Cormorants Preening' by Merridy Cox

Merridy Cox

TO MY DARLING

Falling into a darkness of fear and
despair, you rescue me from a certain
hell, step in and catch me up, give me
your guidance and your trust, and
become my darling,

and then you invite me to leave behind
the land of my birth and all that I have
known and loved, my way of doing and being,

and come with you, holding your hand
and your heart, over a vast unknown ocean

to a land where you can care for me like
a shining jewel forever,

where we can work and play together
and find a certain kind of joy that you
want to share with me,

but where my talents and instincts are of
no value and my efforts are of no avail,

where only you know the map of the
days and nights, where only you can
recognize the threats and the truths,

where I must never look back, never
learn to be except in you, never look for
certainty except in you,

never question your direction or the goal
without consequences of your choosing,

and you know my every hair and hope,
fear and wrinkle,

you know just where I have tried to
conceal a tiny token from my ancestors
or my childhood, even though it is as
insubstantial as a way of placing flowers
by the window,

and just there, in that instant, your
punishment is quick and certain and unrelenting

until I apologize many times, for fear of
being abandoned out here in the part of
the ocean where there be dragons,

and still, I know my world exists, and I
cannot help but live in my world,
evidenced by the clear whistles and
warbles of birds and the rhythmic chirps
of crickets and frogs that are completely
outside your ken because you cannot hear them,

but you deny my world because it is
there, you say, that I am likely to make mistakes;

yet you have no way of getting outside
of yourself, no way of finding empathy
with a place or a person;

nothing exists outside of your universe,

and, conversely, you have no way of
getting into yourself, no way of
recognizing the validity of your soul or
your Creator,

although I have tried, over and over, to
pull at your heart, to open it to the

beauty of both the inner and the outer
worlds, to help you to claim them as
your own, to trust them as the most
valued aspects of yourself,

because without that depth and breadth
of Spirit, my own being is next to dead,
frozen in a painful inaction that benefits
neither you nor me,

but you come back and tell me that I
must be more like you, that you want me
to be a part of you and that I must lose
all softness and all independence to
achieve this, your greatest wish,

and then I try again to tell you that I
have glimpsed sometimes in your hidden
depths the love, joy, and peace that you
have locked away in the darkest corner
of your heart where no one else can see them

and that lock is the complete negation of
this your core, which makes you feel that
something is missing in you, that
perhaps I have the something you need

and to get it you try by turns to deny that
I have it, to punish me for taking it, to
force me to give it to you,

which I cannot do, except to show you
that it is *thee* in your own soul all along,
if you are but a little willing to trust
yourself enough to look and to trust me
to hold you guiltless, my love, while you
stop to examine what it was in your life
that forced you to hide

and to recognize that it was all a
mistake, and that you are not going to be
punished if you accept that Spirit that is
the only thing that ever could join us,

and sometimes a little wave arises in
your depths, and you glimpse it

but then it is gone again, and you feel a
queasy panic

and you hammer shut that inner box with
stronger resolve,

illustrated by yet another command that I
come under your discipline

and I, who was living in a stratosphere
of hope for some seconds, fumble again
at the oars and try again to please you,

but I no longer wish to leave my land for
yours and know that somewhere inside
of me is the strength to tackle my dragons,

just as inside of you is the softness you
need to survive the crashing waves
without being broken,

and I must stop here on this island of
grief and let you get ahead in your own way, darling,

although I still hope that you can see that
it is not Trust that endangers you in your
life, for even though you feel that I have betrayed you,

you know that I cannot commit myself
totally, only because I cannot lose myself:
my spirit does not permit me.

SPRING

Spring Encounter

In a walk down the lane,
an encounter:
the sunlight streams a new dimension
through a ceiling of tall trees in spring bud,
where I meet face-to-face
a tender, translucent green,
broad-leafed maple
sapling.

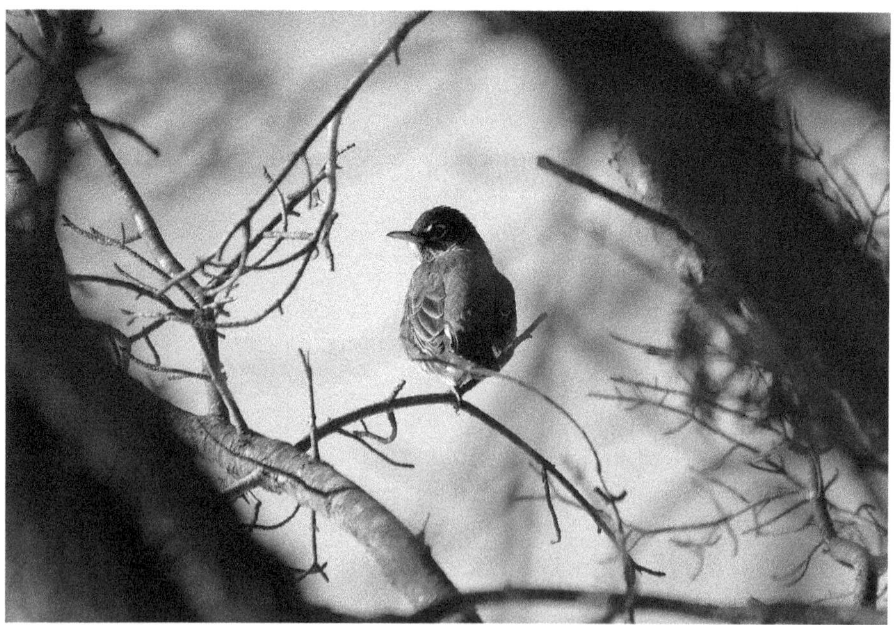

Photograph by Merridy Cox

SUMMER

Summer:

the season of fullness
and joy and peace
when soft clouds
lovingly stroke
sunny, green hills
with their shadow touch,
and the pine and the fir
stand
grouped like school-girls
to sing in the wind
to the music
of distant, clattering cow bells
with a chorus of melodious thrush.

Swaying dandelion clocks proclaim:
"This is summer,"
And life is gentle to all human-kind
in long growing days.

All of us loving the song
and the eternal time
when we are fine-tuned
to play accompaniment
with the cosmos,
and all of us are at one
in the peace and the joy of
Summer.

FALL

Fog

I remember floating
along a path,
through the fog:
a bad dream-like reality,

blind, in spite of straining to see,
I listen to sounds
distorted by mist and
magnified by mind.

Sometimes a tree or bush,
like a familiar ghost,
swirls by, rootless,
into the mist.

Then, that grey building
blocks the way—
concrete but ephemeral—
the fog allowing

only one path to one door,
the fog allowing
no variability and no choice—
and at that moment

an eerie Baskervillian hound
howling,
howling,
to my irrational fear.

WIND

The wind hums endlessly across open fields,
        roars through maples and whines through pines.
It flaps around buildings, creaks along fences;
        it changes sun to shade to sun again
        by pushing cloud here and there.
In the wind, all things can fly;
        birds don't need wings.

The silence of a home,
        white and rug and glass and flowers,
Where music takes over
        and makes noise peaceful:
Here in this small lee of the wind,
        a soul can fold its wings.

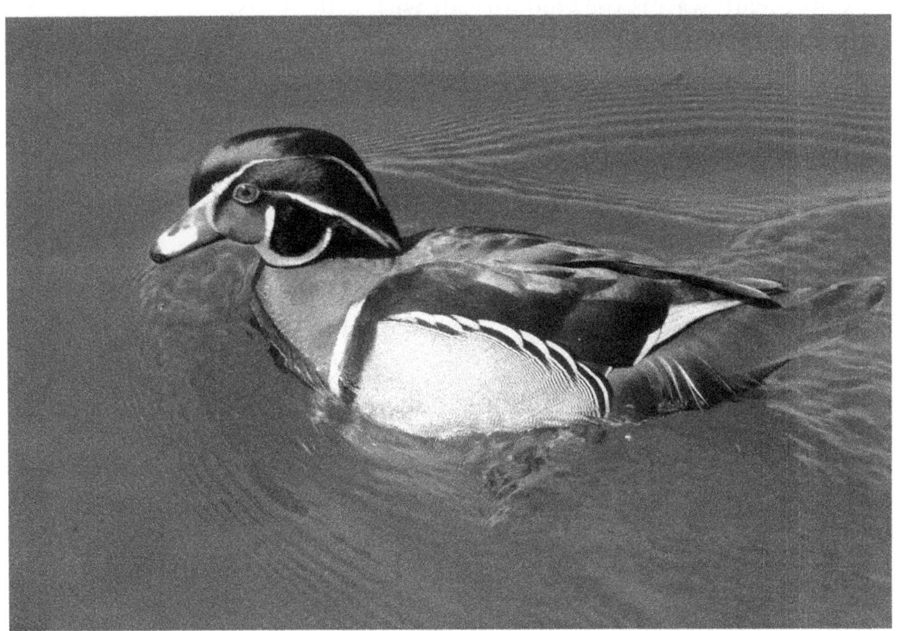

Photograph by Merridy Cox

WINTER

Winter Colours in Canada

Silver ice over water in a swampy lowland pond,
with white snow patches that sparkle sun-stars
to the blue, blue sky.

In between the ice and sky,
green rounded, portly cedars crouch.

And by the pond-side rock we sit on,
little dogwood bushes crowd towards us,
earth-red, bud-tipped branches waiting for spring.

Over there, cattails are translucent yellow
in the sun, no longer seeming dead and dry.

Scarlet berries cling to mountain ash, and
dainty brown cones to black-green fir trees.

Our breath warms the cold, dry air with little mists,
and our fingers curl together in our woollen
hand-knitted mitts.

But, no, we can't feel cold
with the excitement of seeing a jay
as blue as the sky,

or a red fox who quietly watches us,
as we watch him sitting two hill-tops' distant.

What true joy there is in finding in the snow
a magical deer track
or the narrow trail of a lumbering porcupine.

Winter, a blanket of snow, is but
a background for colour and beauty and promise.

MY HOCKEY GAME

I love hockey
Whap, bam!
On the ice

Whap, bam!

And the sound

Whap, bam!

Of the puck

Whap, bam!

On the boards

Whap, bam!

But most of all

Whap, bam!

The sound it makes

Whap, bam!

In the net

Whoosh, clink!

And the cheers

Yeah!
Wow!

And my heart
Whap, bam!

POEM FOR THE GARDEN

Sun, joy of the universe,
Speaks creation.
Water, joy of the earth,
Bubbles blessings.
Life, from sun and water
Loves the green joy of the garden.

—Words written for a plaque in a meditation garden, Ottawa, Canada.

Merridy Cox *is a technical writer and editor who brings clarity to books, academic papers, and government reports and makes them easy for readers. She has been writing poetry for many years. Her* English Manual: Letter by Letter *provides alphabetical tips and tricks on the English language.*
www.englishmanual.wordpress.com *www.facebook.com/merridy.cox.publications*

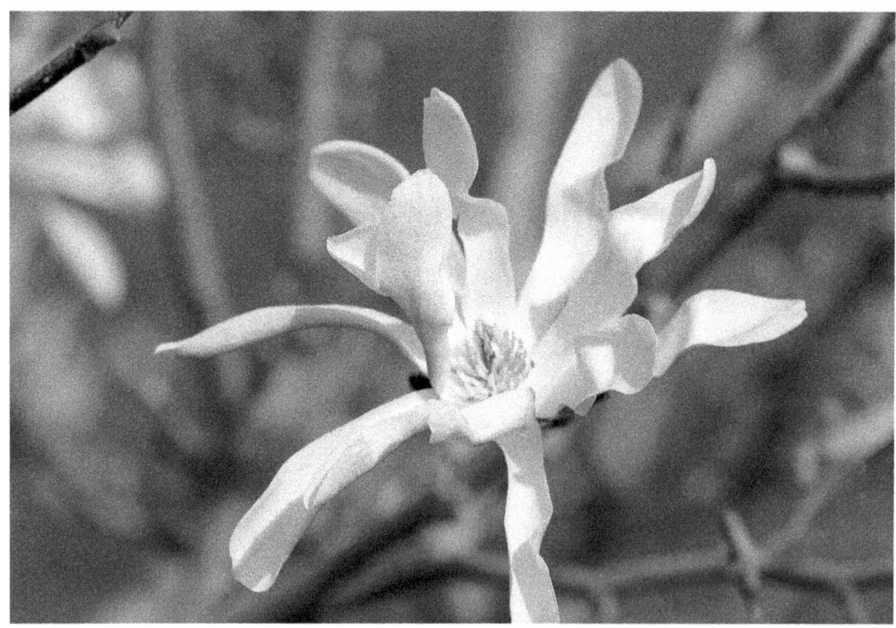

Photograph by Merridy Cox

Susan Munro

HOLY

voice quieted
heart stilled
soul held aloft

He chose to caress me
in my Holy of Holies

where there was no one
to hear my sighs

EVIL

When one knows evil
intimately

There is a greater capacity
to hold light

Tasting evil
is not the same
as swallowing it

FREEDOM

I walked the path less taken
walked most of it alone
many miles, heart shorn thin
to make it to my home

I bore the weight of losing
gave away my heart
gave until there was none left
'cept one bit saved apart

I took this golden nugget
of no vast or earthly worth
buried deep within myself
until there was a birth

With blood and pain and loneliness
travelled distance far
sped through all the universe
on the tail of an exploding star

Met the Ever-Consuming One
on a path not many tread
grew in the face of obstacles
bearing fear, agony and dread

I stopped just once to question
if this was meant to be
the deeply burning answer came
it's the price paid, to be free

***Susan Munro**, a well-known healer and esotericist in the City of Toronto, writes from the gut. Her muse is invited to speak through her voice time and again with a willing surrender. She is the author of two books of poetry:* Coil *published by Bojit Press (2012) and* Ravings of a Lunatic Saint *published by IOWI (2013). Her newest work,* The 8th Interview, *a short novella, is soon to hit the press.*

Saima S. Hussain

I WANT TO RON RON

If dreams were shoes, mine would be a pair of nude-coloured pumps by Christian Louboutin. Known as the Ron Ron, my dream shoes are a size eight; made of shiny patent leather with four-inch heels and the classic round-toe, and of course the designer's signature shiny red-lacquered soles.

This dream of designer footwear is a very recent one. In the past, acquiring any new pair of pretty shoes was a reason to celebrate. Not anymore. Now I am no longer satisfied with good enough; I want the best. And I want it now.

I was raised to be careful with money. My family always lived well but never extravagantly. We bought furniture that would (and unfortunately did) last a lifetime, and quality clothes that became outmoded long before they lost a single stitch. So, when I started working, I never spent more than I had; in fact, I always saved more than I spent. The general rule was to think twice before buying, and two more times after that. Why buy frivolous things, such as expensive shoes and handbags, with money that can be stashed into a savings account? Most of them would go out of style by the end of the season anyway. I was prudent and proud of it. When that rainy day came, I would be ready.

But then, something happened. I packed two suitcases and landed in Toronto. It felt glorious! I had made a decision to embark on a new life and here I was—I had arrived! It took a few weeks for that initial glow to wear off. By then I realised that getting here had been the easy part; the real journey was just beginning.

Like most immigrants, I discovered upon arrival that my slate had suddenly been wiped clean. All the work experience, contacts, and connections that I had cultivated over the years were obsolete. In other words, all my social capital was lost. In a new country I would have to start all over again; rebuild my life, particularly my career, from the ground up. It was going to be an uphill task that would require both time and perseverance. Just how much time and perseverance, I am still finding out almost three years later.

Three years is a long time. Long enough to make me realise that you don't have to wait for good things to happen; sometimes you make them happen. By fulfilling some of my dreams I would give Fortune a nudge and attract success with my positive energy. So, for the first time since arriving in Canada, I dipped into my savings and made a down payment on a Volkswagen Jetta, shiny black and fully loaded with leather seats, power sunroof, and Bluetooth connectivity. I will soon be driving my dream car to my dream job.

Next on my dream list, are my Christian Louboutin shoes. In all their four-inch-shiny-leather-and-red-sole glory, the Ron Ron will be my reward for overcoming the despair of being uprooted and for successfully facing the challenges of rebuilding life here in Canada.

This essay was originally developed at The Shoe Project, which is directed by Katherine Govier, supported by the Mary A. Tidlund Foundation, and hosted by the Bata Shoe Museum.

***Saima S. Hussain** was commissioned to research and write a book about the contributions that were made by Arabs in the fields of medicine, astronomy, arts, education, etc.* The Arab World Thought of It: Inventions, Innovations and Amazing Facts *(Annick Press, Toronto) was published in 2013. That same year, the book won a Best Book award from the Carolina Center for the Study of the Middle East and Muslim Civilization. In 2014, it received an honourable mention at the Arab American Book Awards (Arab American National Museum) in the Children/Young Adult category.*

Janine Georgiou-Zeck

A SIMPLE ACT

Holding hands in the dark
Scared the monsters away
While the world kept on turning
Years passed to today

I'm still looking back
To remember the time
When so simple an act
Could bring peace to our minds

When the world seemed so big
And our part seemed so small
When the danger was real
And we had nowhere to fall

I remember your words
And the touch of your hand
Just a reach
And a kindness to understand

Because you were there
Once upon our time
Your kindness recorded
On my history line

It speaks to my soul when life gets tough
When I feel like I'm falling and the ground is rough
I reach for the memory, with hope I will touch
The hand of my sister, who loved me that much.

LAND OR SEA

She lives in Neverland, he gives it a try
Intrigued by adventures and clear blue skies
He leaped and they flew, sharing all they knew
She opened her heart, forever true
Together they journeyed through waters and lands
Passing their magic to tiny hands
Undefeated by challenges, light was their guide
Occasional storms were not hard to ride

THEN

A ship in the night passed them by
But not before it had caught his eye
A reminder of the un-sailed sea
Of places and people he wished to be
In a solitude boat he took to the water
Not looking back to see the slaughter
Of friendship, courage and balance at sea
Of love everlasting and stability

The magic was lifted no shield in sight
Under attack from left and right
No time for pain, it's time to fight
The land of innocence was no more
Just an empty ocean, and a cold cabin door
She sends out a message by way of wing
Her heart has a stronger song to sing
This ship rebuilt on solid shore
Will not be tipped forever more

FORWARD

Falling forward
Taking a chance
Like a bird from the nest
When he gets his first glance

Tumbling through
Not knowing why
Just hoping when we land
It wasn't too painful to fly

Falling forward
Hoping to gain strength
Expanding our horizons
Into the unknown length

Falling forward
Taking a step at last
Believing what's beyond
Will heal what's in the past

Releasing the chains
Trying again to trust
Courage is a necessity
Faith in yourself, a must

Falling forward
In hope of better days
Fading out the past
In mind, in heart, in ways

PROGRESS

Let's appreciate progress
for what it can do
But let's not get stuck
on a screen with a view

A place yes there is
for the Pods, Pads and Phones
To check in, take photos
and enjoy the fun tones

Life can feel disconnected
even without such devices
How much harder will it be
for the new to survive this

We are fading when we give in
and morph with a machine
We are losing something precious

you know what I mean

I'm going on a diet.
minimal Phone, Pad, TV
I want to see more of my friends face to face
hoping they want to see me!!

Time flies as we stare at screens

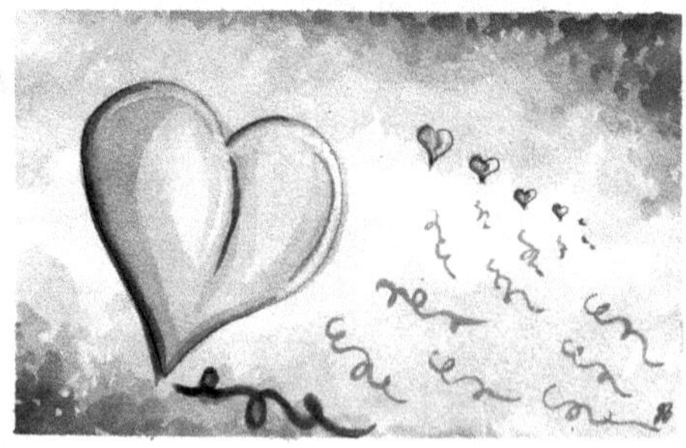

Illustration by Janine Georgiou-Zeck

BROKEN

You built me up,
You held me high,
You lifted my heart
Into the sky.

The seasons changed, so did you.
I could not guess what you would do.
From my place of sweet content,
I did not know what all this meant.

Slowing down to take a glance
at what had got you in a trance.
Fading joy as reality kicks,
life is playing wicked tricks.

No more filled with bliss or joy,
feeling much less than a toy.
Hoping a clearing is in sight,
breathing through what's wrong and right

All my efforts are in vain
as I try to stop the train.
Tearing, ripping us to shreds,
causing turmoil in our heads.

I'm holding fast to memories true,
holding on to what was you.
Before another word is spoken,
have a heart, because mine is broken.

DO YOUR BEST!

When all that you know
is put to the test,
Do your best
Do your best
Do your best!

If it's all that you have
in your box of tools
Whether someone likes it,
or thinks it's not cool.

So many different ways of being
So many different ways of seeing.
Many different shapes and sizes
Many different "realizes"

So many ways to say and do
So many others so unlike you.

With all of the rules, the twists and turns
What are the lessons, that we might learn?

To do as everyone else is doing
or look at our actions
and keep on reviewing.
In every circumstance there's a different true,
a different meaning, a different view.

So don't pull your hair out
because someone was tested,
by an action in which you invested.
Just keep your head,
and consider one's feelings,
and know that it takes
all kinds to do dealings.

Just be gentle and thoughtful wherever you can
speak your mind when needed to stop a bad plan.
Get to know each other but don't lose yourself
be caring and don't put your heart on a shelf.

Be balanced but different and handle with care
anyone who you meet when going out there.
For their journey like yours has its twists and its turns
and we cannot know what will cause them concerns.

Be strong with convictions
to be fair and true,
you may find more in common
with those unlike you.

At the end of the day
When you're ready for rest,
Ponder to yourself,
Did I do my best?

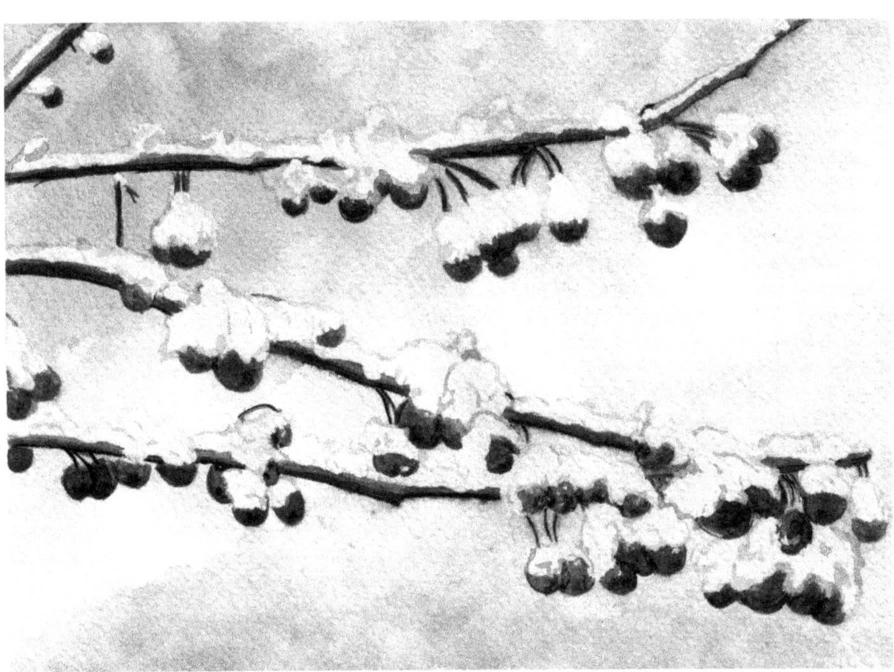

Illustration by Janine Georgiou-Zeck

MY JOSEPHINE

Precious angel gently breathes,
First breaths of life onto my sleeves.

Eyes open up so bright and blue,
perfect smile, light shines through.

You reach for me and now explore.
You're calm, joyful and not a chore.

Before a word, first friend you meet
Receives a hug, and then you greet.

Heart on your sleeve, love abounds,
Happiest with friends around.

Fun loving, thoughtful, kindness and care,
So wise, so young, so gentle and fair.

Truly a daughter any mother would love,
Is my angel girl, sent from above.

Such a child surely must be a dream,
Yet she is not, she's my Josephine.

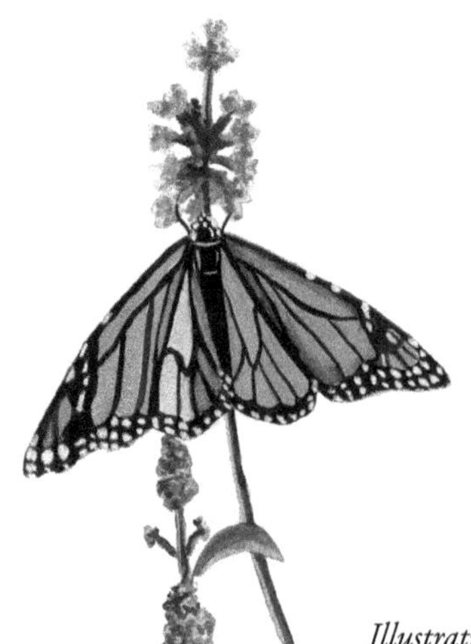

Illustration by Janine Georgiou-Zeck

SUNSHINE

Entered the world, so strong and bright
My little man, my ray of light.
Busy hands and a busy mind,
You're thoughtful, compassionate and kind.

Discovering all there was to see
Your adventures brought treasures to me.

The invisible heart string, I created one day
To keep us close when you're far away.
This will not break no matter how far.
Our love is bonded wherever you are.

My little boy, growing so sublime
Life's an adventure, we fall and we climb
We keep moving forward,
Growing wiser each day.
We discover our path,
We live life our way.

With empathy, dignity, kindness and truth,
With love and integrity, you'll be fireproof.
Keep your chin up and believe in you.
There is no limit to the good you can do.

Jacob, a name of wisdom and strength
Make the most of your life, for its whole length.
Your light shines bright in my heart, you see.
There is no luckier mother than me.

SHE IS ME

The little girl who's reaching for her toy
The little one giggling with joy
The girl with the cute little curls
Who loved her dresses when she twirled.
The sister who loved to hold hands,
And tended to wounds,
The one who understands.

The girl with the tears of pain,
Who fears she will never see them again.
The teen trying hard to fit in,
Who struggles inside her own skin.

The young lady who ventures into the world,
Who sometimes feels thrown and hurled.

The woman who held his hand
The wife who made the promise of eternity,
The woman she didn't know she could be.

The mother who held tender hands
The one who heals the hurts and dries the tears
The one who hopes for their future and eases their fears

She is the woman she hoped she'd be

She is me.

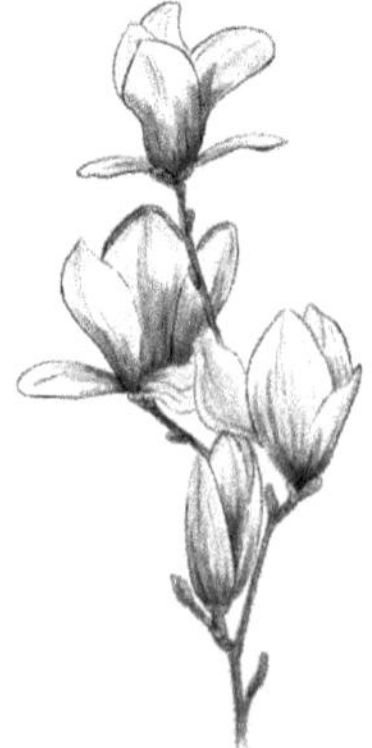

Illustration by Janine Georgiou-Zeck

DO WE?

If something is misplaced, but not truly lost
Do we give up, no matter the cost?

If we have to work, to keep it together
Do we cut our losses, or stay and weather?

If it's time to grow, but one's resisting
Do we let them go, or keep insisting?

If things feel shallow, do we dig deeper?
Push the limits, awaken the sleeper?

__Janine Georgiou-Zeck__ is an artist educator in York Region, owner and program designer at Janine's School of Fine Arts in Newmarket, Ontario. www.jzartstudio.com.

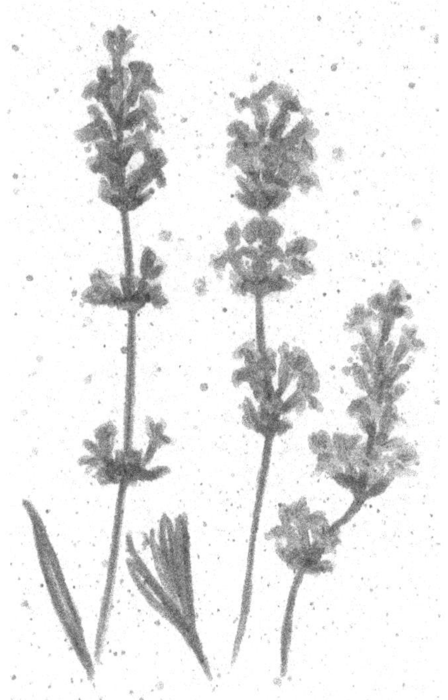

Illustration by Janine Georgiou-Zeck

Rashmee Karnad-Jani

OF STONE TABLES AND BLUE GLASS DISHES

It's January 1st and she's almost at her fifth decade. She's stronger. Thanks to the daily meditation of lying in bed for the first few minutes of wakefulness and counting her blessings—always starting with the children—she knows that she's going to make it through. Well, in some ways she already has.

Her son is smiling more and frowning only sometimes, as does any teenager. He and his sister belt out popular songs as they tidy the kitchen. Her daughter, as serene and strong as all the foremothers whose spirits she carries within her. The cat flops down in the middle of the floor for a belly rub. It's all good.

In a quiet house at breakfast, she chops a nectarine mindfully. Then half a banana, an apple, smallish, and then feeling adventurous, pops half a pomegranate, in memory of Amma's story of Demetre and Persephone.

She decides then that such a magnificent meal deserves the blue glass dish from the neighbourhood of Go Vap outside HCMC, bought long ago. The plate looks like a cupped palm or a large blue strawberry hollowed out.

Armed with a cup of coffee, she makes her way up to her beautiful orange room, thoughtfully decorated by someone who has since decided to move on in a different direction. That's okay, she says to herself and settles her food and drink on the table.

Her stone bistro set. Last summer—at Canadian Tire out for some summery knick knack, grass seed or hedge trimmer—she'd seen it and fallen instantly in love. She wanted the stone and iron table to sit in a sacred space for herself and her loved ones—people who would sit there with her perhaps. She had hesitated, looking at the 200 dollar price tag, the old habit-patterns making her pause and second guess. It was too frivolous, and decadent to boot! Then her daughter's voice whispered in her conscious mind: "You don't have to ask permission or fear raised eyebrows and pursed up looks of disapproval. You make your own money, surely you can afford this." So after a token price check at Home Depot, she'd turned away from the kitschy neon-coloured plastic patio sets to what she now thought of as *her* stone table. She bought it and brought it home. A former student now working at the store helped her load it into her car, quipping about her science class and the homework she'd dish out to her students. Her mood lightened. She'd got some help to fix the table and hoped to have the helper join her there sometime.

But when eyes and hearts are focused on distant visions of peace, they must follow their own path.

That rarely happened as she was relentlessly and consistently cast in the role of a deterrent to *his* peace and *his* tranquil space. He'd never acknowledged the demons that plagued him although he spoke of them in passing. It was always her fault.

On the Monday, she had mentioned her weekend shopping treat to a friend at work who was astute as he was observant.

"Oh, you and your children will have loads of fun meals and long chats at that table," he'd remarked sharing in her pleasure as he admired the photograph. She was surprised that the new void in her life was obvious to many close to her. It was time, she had thought as she waited for him to make his move. He had left three weeks ago. And she hadn't grieved. Not anymore as that was in the past. The grieving was over.

Now the living began.

She had walked through that convoluted time from June until now. And this morning before she made her breakfast, she emptied the closet of old clothes and artifacts of a shared life that can go where they too can be happy.

She sees now that her journal has a bicycle on the cover, a repeated print on every page. So this cold sunshiny January morning, less than a week away from one more wonderful birthday, she sits at her stone table with a pile of fruit in a beautiful blue glass dish, a bag of pens beside her. The children sleep off their joyful revelry of last night, the cat is napping by the window on the other chair, on a mat she's thoughtfully placed there for warmth.

She gives thanks for stone tables and disposable incomes, whispers of strong daughters, blue glass dishes and friends who will want to hear this story of stone tables and blue glass dishes.

FOR ABSHIR, ON THIS SUNLIT DAY

What kind of a world is this
Where young men call their friends in the wee hours
To tell of a brother shot dead at the kerbside?
I find out from an app alert
And hope that it isn't you
Naah, I say. Surely there's more
With your name, Abshir
Though I knew that there's just one you
Who found time to chat between classes
And apologized for a late response to an email
Just a few months ago
I hope and block out
all questions swirling like fallen leaves
through my scattered mind
But confirmations come
"Our Abshir?" I ask. And a response: Yes, our Abshir!
Then the numb hollow in my heart
In this tortured, twisted space
An email mocks me in my inbox,
Your words
"I'll come to your class someday, I promise"

Come to my class today
You did, Abshir
we taught poetry together
Like we'd planned to
Me, trapped in this heavy cage of bones
And you, a wisp of mist this sunshine day
already a memory

What kind of place is this?
Where we mourn young men dead before their time
What kind of place is this?

My friend and classmate Abshir Hassan was killed on July 8th, 2014.

DARK SKY MOMENTS

Class dismissed
Day plans for the morrow
Beckoned and working through
I noticed the light dim
Behind trees of our Cdwd forest
Baarish! My heart leapt
And I came back to the moment
It's not *baarish*, silly
It's not the monsoon
This is Markham not Mumbai
And I smiled, sighed
That I have two homes now
And I belong in both
With fierce unapologetic, undiluted love
The grey sky shone
With blessings

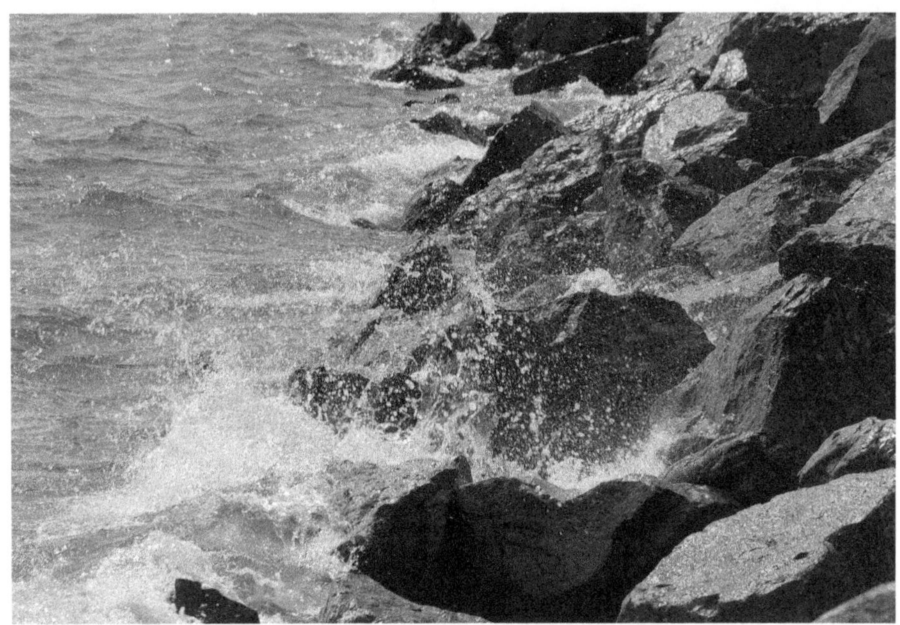

Photograph by Merridy Cox

MY DEFICIT LIST

I come with very little
Haven't skied downhill
Nor snowboarded
Skates aren't for me
Neither are beaver tails
I come with very little

Haven't cheered at hockey games
Guzzled beer at dawn
Or been to The Cottage
I come with very little

I just have my memories
Of an ancient Land
Memories of smudging snowshoes
And Grandfather Teachings
Honouring the land and reading the stars
For signs of travel
And of being Me

those who came after
Have others of *mogra* and *mungphali*
Sitar and *savera,* ghazals and Goa
Boat rides in Nha Trang
Sentosa sunsets, Dharavi tears and Naigaum rain
Lucknow kurtas and K Rustom icecream
Parsi Dairy *ni* lassi and Swagat *bhel*
Amma's fish curry and Kavlem peace
I
come
With
Very
Little
You think?

And I chuckle and shake my head
At how little you know of other worlds.

DAFFODIL LANDSCAPES

To all of us
Who trudge through
And walk weary steps
Wake another day
And wonder whether and if
Or when
better days
Will ever come

I share this Gujrati saying
Strange as it's a language
that
has caused me
Great joy and pain
yet sums it up
quite nicely

Kadhyaa etlaa
kaadhvaana nathi!

So trudge one more day
And celebrate the sun
Still high in the west sky, late
Promises that the Wordsworth landscape
Is always in our hearts
That will soon dance with
The daffodils

BLACK BEADS AND GOLDEN LIGHT

She scrambled to get dressed this morning. The lawyer had sent her the final draft of the separation agreement the day before and she had spent time printing out a copy to read at work so that she didn't soil her cozy, cluttered home with the demands and numbers, cutting off and letting go—that this whole process entailed. Full and final settlement of dues and complete severance of ties legally, seemed a lot to process when all around her were reminders of a life she'd tried to create for them and their children.

She hurried into her room which had been for a few days a dressing room, temporarily used for clothes. She stuck her hand into the dresser drawer and pulled out a simple necklace to wear with the bright yellow *kurta* she had chosen. A tightly coiled rope of black beads threaded beautifully by unknown fingers with a small golden pendant of the goddess Lakshmi, the giver of wealth. Tarnished as it was, after years of being shuttled around between the many homes they'd lived in together, it still brought a flood of memories of Parel, Dadar, Pune, Girgaum. A traditional Marathi *mangal sutra* she was trained to associate it with the symbol of a woman's marital status. Hurried though she was, her eyes pricked with sudden tears as she, for a moment, burdened by the *tsk tsk* of long ago voices, questioned her right to wear jewelry that only adorns the necks of married women.

I'm in some kind of limbo she thought. Not married, nor widowed. "Not yet picked" and "poor thing he had no choice over Death." These situations were somehow preferred to what she was about to become: a wife "left" by the man she'd married. "Surely he made that choice. Such a nice fellow too. I wonder what happened. Do you think...? Well you know what they say about strong women." Post-mortems were inevitable.

Then in that split second she remembered what she'd said to her mother when her father had died almost three decades ago. Hoping to prevent her from sinking forever into a widow's garb, she had said: "You didn't make this happen. He died and that's true. It's not your fault. You can keep living your life with joy and loving the colours you want. You can thread through your hair the jasmine you buy so lovingly for me." She had been twenty-one then and already knew this. Women are required by traditional society to wear labels that proclaim their possession by the man they stand beside. "So what if he died. You did your best. You live on, Amma," she had said to her mother then.

The long-ago girl she had been then whispered the same words in her ears this morning. She had been the spunky sunshine that reminded her to breathe as her world had begun to unravel in the last few years.

That long-ago girl persisted and whispered: "Remember what you'd told your mother long ago. You can't forget that now."

She smiled then, this silver-haired woman. She straightened her spine, shook off the cobwebs from her heart. She sifted through the thoughts that were the lived realities of many women in many places. Her own was different. In a drawer full of necklaces, coloured glass from Fabindia, wood, shells, twisted metal, mother of pearl with a starfish embedded at the centre: each piece had its story, some hers and some inherited. She didn't need only black beads to define her. She had all the colours of the rainbow to celebrate her journeys.

She shrugged her shoulders. When you have a job to do, a doctorate to earn, children to raise and sunflowers to grow, there's no time to mope and feel sorry for yourself.

She shook out her still-wet hair that smelt of jasmine flowers and Goan *vovlaan*, defiant and serene at once. She then slipped on the necklace, adjusted the bead on the fastener, fed the cat, and let herself out. She locked the door carefully behind her.

She'd have a wonderful day she promised herself.

True that! She photographed sunflowers that evening. And clouds. She came home to her son and a cup of tea.

***Rashmee Karnad-Jani** is the first born daughter of Veena Hattangadi and Bhaskar Karnad of Udipi and Dharwad, India. She's a keen observer of the goings-on in her everyday life. She was born in Mumbai and raised in Goa. She has a bachelor's degree in science, a degree in education. She also holds specialist qualifications in adolescent literacy and special education from York University. She is currently completing her Master's degree in education. Rashmee is an advocate of social justice, raising awareness of children and women's rights, environmental sustainability as well as equitable educational outcomes for students with learning disabilities. Rashmee speaks six languages and writes in English, Hindustani, and Marathi. She writes from a place of deep mindfulness and asserts that her writing emerges as a stream of spiritual consciousness in a given moment.*

SONNETS

I – NATURE'S GREATER THAN ART

They have praised Niagara Falls and its dower
Artists, lovers, rope-walkers, writers, priests
All awed by your majesty and power
All vowed to return for other trysts

I have been at your shrine for myriad years
Annually, biennially, once in a while
Expecting to look at your face in tears
If you have changed as little as my smile

But No! You have not changed. Time has only
Made you more mysterious, memorable
Your beauty more enticing, famously
Is this why you keep flowing as able?

Keats' ode on the urn is frozen in art
But Nature is greater for beating heart

II – ROSES AND ROSES AND ROSES

In Butchart Gardens the roses bloom deep
In yellows, reds, whites and pinks they diffuse
Heady fragrances that readily sweep
Over hosts of visitors to amuse

One hundred and thirty varieties grow
On that quarried land in Victoria west
With loving tender care they stand aglow
Exulting in Nature's bounty with zest

Manicured plants and bushes also stand
To feast one's eyes at symmetry of art
A man-made human enterprise at hand
Not to rival Nature but to be part

Those flowers and roses give such beauty
To garden shows grown from sense of duty

III – THE BOND

Marriage of true love unlike what the Bard
Said admits of sundry impediments
Of changing interest, age and health marred
As the years take wing through life's sentiments

Still marriage in twentieth century dear
Has disdained intimate habitation
In search of personal freedom for fear
That same life might leave them behind station

Yet in such pursuit of merry-go-round
Love itself has taken its lumps hands down
When too late the partners hear the true sound
Of that first love that their marriage did crown

Love has always stood up in face of fond
Expected changes to keep strong the bond

IV – A POPE LIKE HIS NAMESAKE

To serve the people of God a priest should
Lead with his heart not head most of the time
For which deep and searching formation would
Do well in seminaries that don't mime

To wake up the world with their work with poor
To preach the message of Christ the priest needs
Genuine compassion willing to be doer
To care for the spirit of man and deeds

The modern Church racked with scandals galore
Can't hide behind complex clericalism
Certain cronyism and careerism more
Pope Francis told superiors with realism

We are all sinners but not all corrupt
Sinners are accepted, Pope was abrupt

V – WRITERS AND DRINK

Myth there is of writers who drink and write
Fostered by images of Hemingway
Fitzgerald, Cheever and Chandler all right
To boost sales of Scotch, rye and bourbon say

Many a young and ambitious scrivener
Thus has taken to booze to inspire him
To create that great novel, a sure winner
To bring him fame and glory to the brim

Fact is writers drink after their writing
To relieve tension of creativity
Upon revisions work of polishing
Goes to editors to make it pretty

Still the myth endures surely it must be
To fool newbies with false ideas you see

VI – COMMON INTEREST KEEPS FRIENDS

Books have been written on how to make friends
And influence people but not what keeps them
Talk about the other and he sure bends
His ear like one truly possessed with gem

Smile and the world will smile back says the book
Cry and you cry alone with no friend near
You may like ice cream but want fish to hook
Then give the fish a worm not cream my dear

Best way to win an argument is not
To enter it or avoid it like snakes
If you want to gather honey, big shot
Don't throw stones at beehives, do what it takes

All this friendly counsel is good and fine
Although common interest keeps friends in line

VII – SALOME'S DANCE

Can mother and daughter lust for same man?
It would depend on the man and his fate
In Herod's time a man named John began
To carp Herod for bedding brother's mate

A furious Herodias wanted John killed
But Herod was afraid, for people loved
The prophet John the Baptist with grace filled
Sent him to jail instead to please beloved

On Herod's birthday daughter Salome
Danced her heart out to trance him to rapture
As gift the king would grant Salome's plea
She asked for John's severed head from capture

Thus the mother wreaked her hateful revenge
With help of daughter just glad to avenge

VIII – SUMMER TIME

Summer time and the living is easy
That is if you live like Porgy and Bess
In Deep South with no care and not busy
Just carousing around with no address

Up in the North in the cottage country
Summer time is for lazing on the deck
Watching boats zoom on the lake aplenty
And loons gliding to land on water's back

In the city with backyards smelling sweet
Under maple shade with barbecue on
It's time for family and friends to greet
Share food and drink while kids frolic on lawn

Yes, summer time passes quickly like pleasure
So make the best of this annual treasure

IX – SIMPLY AWESOME

Palazzo Madama in Torino
Harbours seventy thousand works of art
From Gothic, Renaissance, Baroque but lo!
Most mesmerising of them all apart

A scene of life-sized sculptures depicting
Jesus Christ lowered down from Cross yet raised
Above ground in fine symmetry showing
Magdalene, Mary, Salome all dazed

Upright Joseph of Arimathaea
Apostle John, Nicodemus convey
Pathos and movement that inspired artist
To craft in such imaginative way

If art could show path of faith to people
This sculpture rises to rank of steeple

X – HAIKU VERSUS SONNET

While Shakespeare put his mark on the sonnet
With a rhyming couplet made it English
Basho in Japan began with cold sweat
To compose haiku verses in anguish

Emotion of love inspired English bard
Lack of emotion guided the haiku
The sonnet with fourteen lines kept the guard
Only five syllables saw haiku through

Figurative language, metre and rhyme
Carry the sonnet to poetic fancy
Simplicity and distance haiku prime
Invite the reader to be its patsy

Thus the old become relevant again
To give voice and meaning to new refrain

Ben Antao *was born in Goa, India, and has been a journalist, teacher, writer and a certified financial planner, now living in Toronto, Canada. He graduated from the University of Bombay (M.A. in English) and worked as a reporter for* The Navhind Times, *Panjim, Goa (1963-64) and later joined* The Indian Express *(1965-66) in Bombay as a reporter. In 1966, he was awarded a journalism fellowship by the World Press Institute based at the Macalester College, St. Paul, Minn., for a year's study and travel in the United States. He has published five novels, two memoirs, two travelogues as well as several short stories. His recent book of short stories is titled* The Concubine and Selected Stories.

Fran McEvoy Clare

TIME …

Sam plays 'As time goes by'
And Ingrid Bergman starts to cry
The old say "time goes too fast"
The lover hopes this time will last

Some in time set their spirit free,
Some spend time writing poetry
Some waste time searching for 'more'
Some misuse time to go to war

Prisoners 'do' time
Clock watchers 'watch' time
Too many say they 'have no time'
Too few give others the gift of their time

Cherish time as it ticks away
Soon today will be yesterday
No matter what you think or do
Make every moment count for you

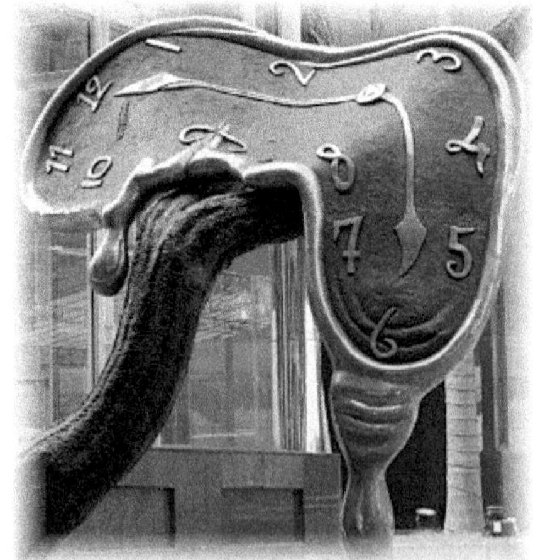

Photograph by Alvin Brown

CHOICES

Something more
Something less
Second chance
Second guess

Blurred vision
Crystal clear
Hopeless and forgotten
Remember my dear

The end of a chapter
First page of a book
Lost souls
Optimistic outlook

Sleeping baby
Restless minds
Selfish thought
Always kind

Doing what's right
Telling a lie
Laughing out loud
Having to cry

Never ending
Never begun
Nobody
Everyone

Feeling lonely
Having friends
Yes definitely
It depends

OPTIMISTIC

Sad and down
Choice is made
Helpless frown

Lost and confused
Future bright
A beacon to follow
Lost in flight

Full of joy
A heavy heart
Failing to try
Studying smart

Endless love
Unfulfilled desire
Giving up
All you aspire

Choices we make
Every day of our lives
Find your courage
To live—not just survive

NATURE'S PALETTE

Peel back the grey and see what you find
Nature's colorful palette hiding behind

Tall buildings and people trapped in web clichés
Nature calls you to escape technology's maze

Our world is linked with computer hypertext
We rush through the 'now' to see what comes next

With bits and bytes we have become a little lost
Nature's waiting in colors, gentle and soft

Nature's twitters and webs are from birds and spiders
But slowly she's becoming an impoverished outsider

We are now a race of web designers and bloggers
We are texting junkies and plugged in joggers

Blackberries and apples, no longer picked but for chats
They display virtual friends and our Google facts

But nature is relentless and even though we are wired
She keeps sharing her beauty and hopes we're inspired

Take a minute to embrace all that nature supplies
Close your computer and open your eyes

There is abundance of beauty if we stop and pause
Take a break from your iPad, unplug your iPod

To navigate her beauty you don't need G.P.S
Take a stroll through the park and enjoy her finesse

Enjoy a cluster of color instead of your database
Nature is calling and will fill your heart space.

BUBBLES

If I chose another shape I'd like to be round
I'd choose to be a Bubble and I wouldn't touch the ground
I'd sparkle in the sun and float through the air
With the whole world I'd choose my beauty to share

I'd dance through the atmosphere and in the sunshine
I'd show the world the glory of color that is all mine
I'd glisten and travel to pastures of green
I'd be the most beautiful bubble anyone had seen

When everyone is sleeping and it's dark at night
I'd fly to Australia like a colorful kite
Because in the darkness I would find it difficult to glow
So to the sunshine is where I would have to go

I'd float to where there are valleys and flowers
Wherever there is sunshine I'd stay for 24 hours
My array of colors: magenta, golden yellows and blue
Would reflect the world's magic in a marvelous hue

I would collect all the laughter from children at play
I would gather tears of joy that spill through the day
I would soak up the feelings from hearts that are in love
I would listen to secrets not usually heard of

I would caress the lonely and help the sad find hope
I would join the wedding party of those who eloped
I would whisper to the old there is still beauty within
I would soothe crying babies while in the air I would spin

For teenagers, I would show them it's not as hard as it seems
For unhappy middle-aged couples, I'd wish them new dreams
For the sick and the dying, I'd give them solace in sleep
For those suppressed, I'd wipe away tears that they'd weep

And when my job is done in the daylight sublime
I'd 'pop' myself off to another space and time
Because bubbles don't just burst we continue as stars
We join the planets of the universe and shine just like Mars

We shine then at night in the darkness we once thought cold
We radiate all that we gathered on earth and let it unfold
We give you back the love, happy feelings and joyful tears
Stars are just bubbles and we shine for millions of years

So if I could be another shape I'd definitely choose "round"
I'd choose to be the most beautiful bubble ever to be found
I'd choose to float through the air and then shine every night
I would shine, not just beauty, but God's glorious light.

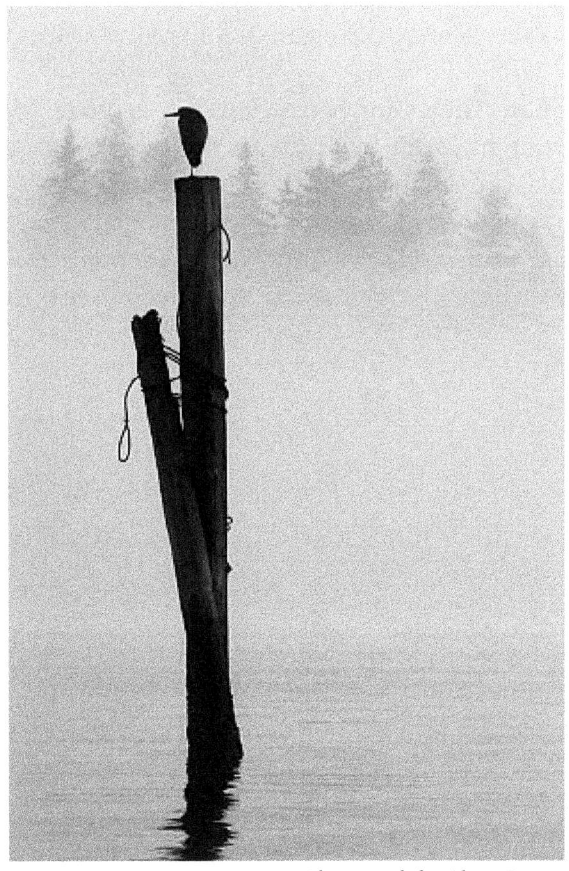

Photograph by Alvin Brown

NOW

Now that I am old I depend upon you more
You are my memory, I don't recall the day before

Now that I am fragile I need you to hold me near
You are my muscles that are aged beyond their years

Now you are my logic whenever I become confused
You seem to accept what I chose to refuse

Now you are my intellect that I have in time forgot
You are my shoulders that carry worries I do not.

Now you are my solace when I know and understand
You are my calm and my courage when I hold your hand

Now you are my friend, my partner my love, my wife
You are part of my 'being,' you are one with me in life
Now I need to tell you because over fifty years
We have loved and lived, through happy times and tears
Now I would thank you but I know words are not required
You are my life, my joy, my passion and true love inspired.

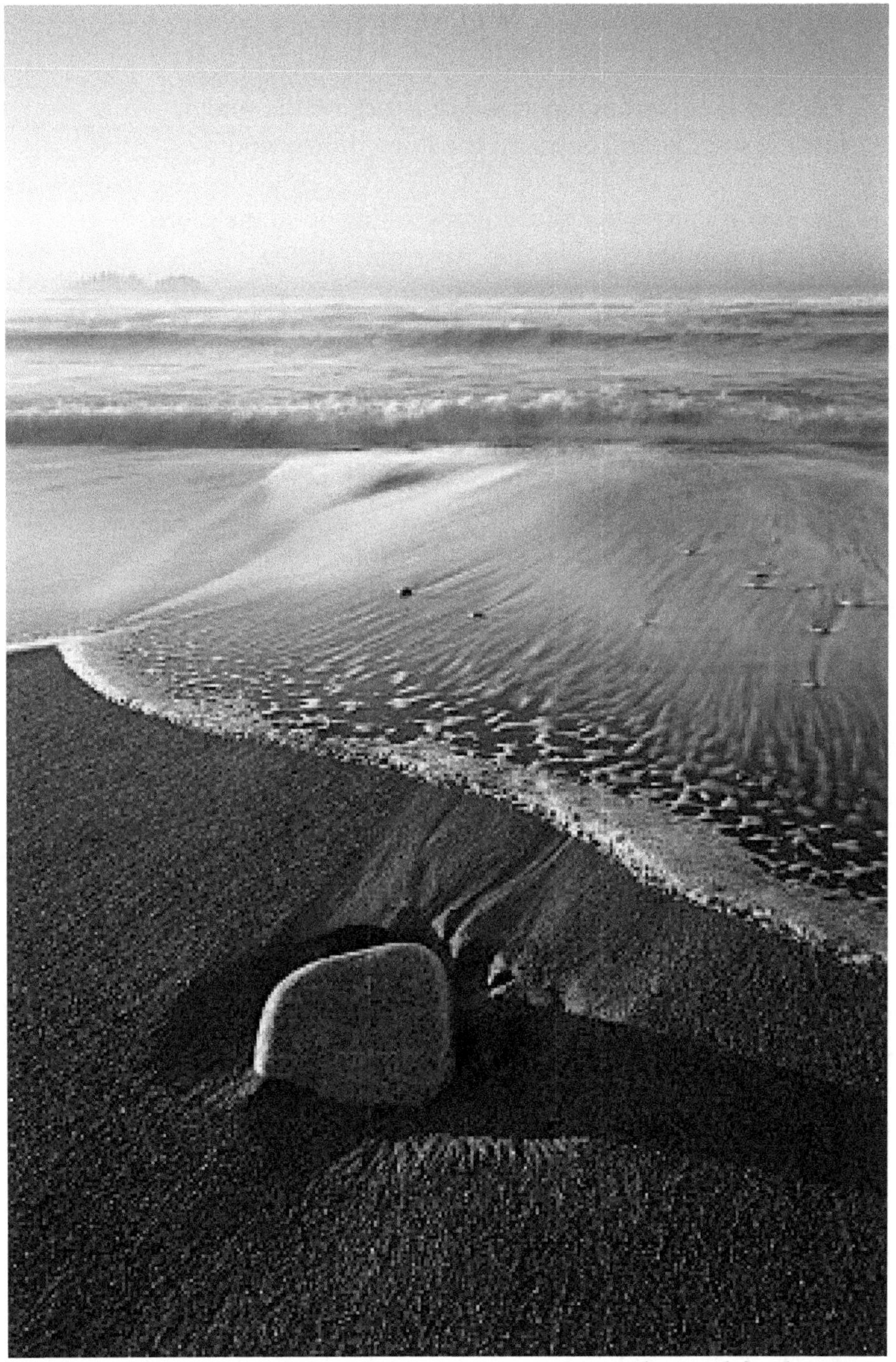

Photograph by Alvin Brown

WHAT IF?

You may say "Nothing special. Just a rock on the strand,
Just the sun filtering down on the stony brown sand"

You say "It's just water and stones washing up to the shore
I've seen photographs like this many times before"

What if you are heartbroken, here to bid lost love goodbye
And the water streamed from the tears that you cried?

What if you are a parent whose child has just died?
And the rock is all the 'tomorrows' your child is denied?

What if you are a husband who just lost his wife?
And together you watched such sunrises in life?

What if you loved here and here felt your first kiss?
What if you laughed here with someone you now miss?

The sun glistens on the water as it reaches the shore
Can you see clearly now what you couldn't see before?

Shadows of love lost, sorrow and pain?
Dwell a moment, take a close look again...

What if the ripple of waves are life's second chance?
And in the waves' motion you felt you could dance?

What if that sky with its magnificent hue
Promised hope and joy in all things you do?

What if the rock framed by the waves washing in,
Was as powerful as the life you are about to begin?

What if the grains in the sand and the pebbles on shore
Are the feelings of hope you never imagined before?

What if you pick up the rock and take it home?
Would the magic of others' dreams be with the stone?

As you look at the photograph and enjoy the horizon
Do you realize this is beauty your heart soars upon?

But, what if it was "Just a rock on the strand?
Just the sun filtering down on the stony brown sand"

Isn't there magic in this moment captured in time?
What if you opened your mind to all that's sublime?

What if you let your imagination run free?
And this rock and this water was more than great photography?

Fran McEvoy Clare
Fran is passionate about everything she does in life. She loves travelling, cooking, and philosophy, bringing joy and a creative touch to everything she does from dancing in the kitchen to philosophic poetic musings.

Nadia Tretikov

OUR FIRST LOVE

All surrounded by eternal beauty,
Being captured by the wind of love,
It is resting on a weightless cloud,
In between sparkly-silver doves.

What is lost—is lost forever,
What is gone—never comes again,
But the love—given once in heaven,
Lasts forever in a pure heart.

MY SUNSHINE

You are my Angel from the skies,
You are my magic mirror vision,
My golden sunbeam high above.

You are my silky velvet summer,
And winter snow, white and bright,
You are my chiming silver raindrops,
My stream through milky morning mists.

You are my happiness,
You are my sunshine,
You are my soul,
Having rest within.

FAITH

I see the people marching in lines,
I see them tied up by invisible ties,
I see them looking all the same way,
I hear them whooping all the same…

They are fully fed and nicely dressed,
But there is no joy in their faith,
Like some enormously greedy beast
Took all their hearts and made a great feast.

How long will it take?
How much will it cost?
To fill in the gap,
And to break this black curse?

LOOK INSIDE YOU

Look deep inside you,
What do you see?
The wind blowing alongside the sea?
The mountains going up to the skies?
The rivers running from side to side?

Do you see anything strange to yourself?
Maybe the dust? Or maybe the shell
Which is the size of a little black pin,
Shrinking and shrinking all ways endlessly?

Maybe it's time
To open the gates and
Let some fresh air in,
To smash it all away.

Coolness and heartlessness,
Arrogance too—
Look all around you!
Look inside You!

DAZZLING LIGHT

What a great joy it is to see Dazzling Light,
Giving the strength to glide way up high!
Giving the strength to resist the black night,
Covering everything from the deepest inside.

What a great joy is to feel wings alive,
Reaching the stars and touching the sky!

Can you imagine this?
Have you ever tried?
To fly like an angel?!
To soar in the sky?!

TO THE TEACHER

So many years to refer,
So many doubts still prefer,
But very deep inside your soul,
There is Great Trust, as good as gold.

Don't let the cruelty crash it down.
Do you remember what it means "to be proud?"
This word is for you.
Keep the banner high,
Your light is in the eyes,
That look so open-wide;
Your knowledge is the best of guides,
Your virtues are your solutions' line.

Great joy is waiting for your heart;
Is it hard to believe in this? Feel alive!
That joy will melt the ice of fears,
Sweep all the scars from inside tears.
Your life—your dreams,
Just turn around and look inside you,
And be proud.

YOUR LIVES

If you travelled once far above
The horizons of the human mind,
You will always remember everything,
From the hundreds of those lives.

One can say: "I remember everything"
The other will only smile.
One can say: "Not a problem, I know this"
The other will ask: "Have you tried?"

We go in this life through everything,
Beginning with the littlest lie,
We are roaming through the darkness
Of consciousness and brutality falls inside.

One step, one invisible barrier,
Lies between us and Eternal Life;
One can say: "I remember everything"
The other will only smile.

The miracles are all around us—
The sunrise and the birth of a child—
Whoever remembers everything
Will close his eyes and fly…

NEVER TOO LATE

It is never too late to change yourself,
It is never too late to begin,
It is never too late to stop yourself,
It is never too late to live,
It is never too late to fulfill your dreams,
It is never too late to love,
All you need is to look at everything,
With the eyes of Eternal Life.

BLOCKED

"Why are you here?" asked the pilgrim.
"What are you doing here, so far away?"
I was looking at him and he seemed very familiar…
But where have I seen this tarnished look?
I couldn't remember. I kept silent.

"Go away! It's not the place for a scoundrel. Out!"
Glancing at him again, I saw in his look—myself.
I turned around and dragged myself away,
but the question was there:
Where?

My thoughts were racing,
Looking for the way out.
I was drawn by the wind to the ocean,
the rocky waterside that happened to be there.
"Stop!"

It followed me everywhere, that voice and that look!
My thoughts were rushing. I wanted to go back.
To my life in the colours of the rainbow,
to my home, and to my child.
But my thoughts were rushing,
and the voice next to me was screaming,
"Halt!"

MARY

Mary stood still in full darkness, trying to understand what just happened. All of a sudden, an arch appeared in front of her, covered with garlands of beautiful flowers. It was hard to imagine how they could so flawlessly be arranged on it. Charmed, Mary went closer and the scents filled her lungs, intoxicated her heart.

Carefully, she stepped inside the arch and in that instant found herself in a tunnel, on both sides of which, through a milky-cloudy haze were outlined the contours of closed doors. Mary held off, hesitating—which one of them? Her attention fell on the empty far corner of the wall, and her arm involuntarily stretched forward.

Bedazzling her with unusually bright light, the door burst open. An unexplained feeling of joy and happiness swept over her. Straight to her feet were falling streams of a cascading waterfall, and she instantly wanted to plunge herself into it. Scooping a handful of water, Mary splashed it onto her face, again and again.

The water was crystal clear and cool. Mary placed herself in the soothing stream of cleansing beauty. Her body luxuriated and freshened. After splashing to her heart's content, the girl exposed her body to the warmth of the sun and with unusual lightness climbed up and seated herself on a rocky ledge by the waterfall. The sun was greeting her.

Delighted, Mary stood up and headed to the riverside, softly making her way through silky grass. Soon, she was in an orchard full of unusual, colourful fruits.

Even without tasting them, she already felt their life-giving strength. She stood on tiptoe and gently lifted an apple. It easily came away in her hand, honey-gold and deliciously flavourful. She had eaten one of these before, but where? Of course, in her childhood, in her grandfather's orchard! In a couple of minutes there were only a few seeds left in her hand, which were immediately picked up by birds coming in from behind her back. The birds were not afraid of her—everything existed as one whole world.

The girl wanted to try one more unusual fruit that attracted her with its bright appearance. The taste was absolutely exceptional: soft, jelly-like, slightly reminding her of the flavour of wild raspberry and strawberry. Holding it in her hands, she was slurping up the sweet, juicy flesh. "Heavenly!" thought Mary, but then: "Where am I?"

She wanted to stay in this wondrous garden, filled with birdsong and cool shade. At that instant, next to her, under a grand apple tree, she saw a large wicker chair. Mary sat comfortably in the chair, closed her eyes and took a deep, restful breath.

The light breeze carefully touched her lips, cheeks, eyes, as if trying to grasp her features. Picking up her hair, it blew it around, messed it up, softly placed it back down on her shoulders and joyfully it whirled around. It was a dance of love—gracious and slightly naughty, caressing and provocative.

Mary never felt anything like that. She was dashing to the tops of the trees, flying up to the clouds, dropping down like lightning onto rippling waters, swirling in the vortex of wild dance, rejoicing and triumphing, winning and loving, liberating and celebrating. She wanted it to never end, but she knew that was impossible.

All of a sudden the wind was still, then, shooting past again, beckoned her to follow. Reluctantly, Mary stood up, confused, and took a step. She passed a green meadow, crossed a rushing stream, and bending down, made her way through a thicket of shrubs and quickly climbed to the top of a hill.

The scenery was breathtaking. She was standing on the edge of a cliff. In front of her, there lay the universe, immense and incomprehensible and mysterious!

She saw stars and planets and moons. And among them, very small, she saw the Earth. The wind pushed her slightly forward.

Down there, there was that beautiful arch covered with garlands of flowers and the door that she had once seen in her dreams. The door leading her home! Mary paused, trying to remember forever everything she saw.

The Earth was waiting for her with the freshness of morning, the chirping of birds, the clear stream of water and the rainbow, with scarlet-red sunset, and necessarily, absolutely necessarily, with that gentle and tender breeze…

SPRING CLOUDS

The Two froze in wonder—there was Spring on Earth. Birds sang, trees blossomed, and children filled the playgrounds. Dogs, set free, mingled among them. Excited, the children hugged and kissed the dogs, who in turn wiggled their tails, barked happily and licked the kids' faces with their rough and wet tongues.

The grass was freckled with dandelions. Somewhere in the shade under the big spruces flocked forget-me-nots, the colour of the sky. Up and down the trails, the cyclists swept along.

Keeping watch over the busy life below, the Two, taking turns, played 'Right or Wrong':

"Is he going to win?" asked the one.

"No!" said the other.

"Wrong!" said the one.

"Are they going to fall?" said the other.

"Yes," said the one.

"Right!" said the other.

They wanted to be down there so much. They wanted to spread out on the green grass and rest in the sun.

Suddenly, the Two saw an "unusual silhouette." Someone was moving very slowly, making short stops and looking around.

All the hustle here and there was not for him. He came near the apple tree, covered with snow-white blossoms, very slowly crouched underneath and clicked with the button of his camera. Click!

Surprised, the Two scattered apart.

"Has he noticed us?"

"Of course, he did."

Click! The one of the Two blinked with his invisible eyelashes and blushed.

"He can't see us, can he?"

"You're silly! He is only a human!"

"Yes, but the camera!"

"No, he can't. They are not that advanced."

Both became silent again. The man neared the little pond in the park and cautiously sat on the ground. Click! Little frogs shot like the stars of fireworks in different directions. The camera produced a cascade of snaps. The clouds burst with laughter.

It was a nice spring day… They wanted to be on Earth so much!

MY STAR

The clouds, you tell me,
Where is my Star?
Behind the high mountains?
Behind the horizons far?
Behind the deep oceans?
Behind the almighty winds?
Does it wait for me?
My Star that always exists!

Mary was sitting still on the front veranda of the house. The evening quietude entranced her. The sky was studded with stars. Her eye captured their live dance. First, it seemed that it was only her imagination that the stars were "talking," sparkling to her with their bright "smiles."

Suddenly, among this unusual abundance of the living world, she noticed a beam, leading straight down to her. Not knowing why, Mary kneeled. She felt very vividly that it was her Star.

The gleam, falling straight to her feet, turned into an ascending ladder. An instant of hesitation—and she stepped up: first carefully, then more hardily and joyously. Finally, she is on the peak, somewhere very, very high. She can hardly see the Earth, so far left behind, wrapped in the ocean of stars, meteorites and space dust. Mary was about to take a step and felt the rocky surface. She saw rather than felt—it was a planet! Yes, it was a new planet.

Mary was looking for a paradise garden, but saw nothing except craters. The planet was absolutely 'naked.' Suddenly, she noticed right in front of her a mountain flower of unusual beauty.

Before her eyes, the flower made its way through the rocky crust—the planet was greeting her. Thrilled, Mary leaned forward and touched it. The flower flew off the ground towards her.

Turning back, she saw a green meadow. How? She stepped on soft, golden-green grass—a little island of emerging life. That was her planet, that was her Star...

It was time to go back to Earth. Taking a last glance at her future home, Mary carefully took a step back, onto the same ladder which appeared in the darkness. The last step—and she was again on the veranda.

The strange feeling wouldn't leave her for a long time. Home... Now she knew what it meant.

The Star, sending her its light, stays in her mind always. It doesn't disappear. It follows her everywhere. It is in every moment of her life, always with her—Home.

Nadia Tretikov *was born in the Ukraine. She is a published author of poems and short stories, including one thriller* The Running Elephant, *published in Russian, by Toronto Media in 2003. This anthology is her first publication in English.*

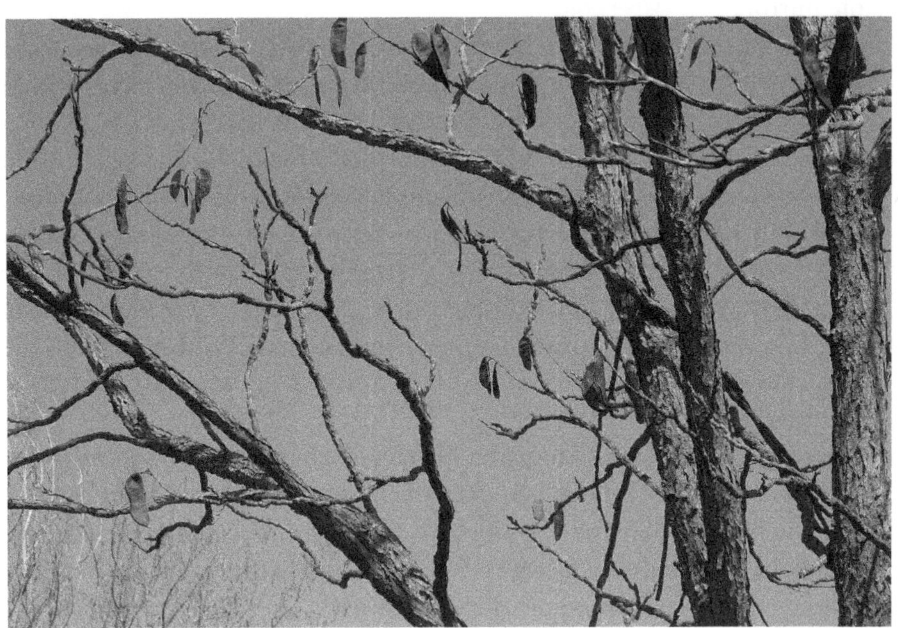

Photograph by Merridy Cox

Mary Ellen Koroscil

WEAR YOUR GLASSES IN THE HOT TUB

Escaping from the city for a few days is always a treat. My boyfriend and I arrived at a resort that was lifted from the pages of a fifties travelogue. It was obviously a motel offering rustic appeal, though it wasn't quite described that way in the online "Deal of the Week." It was cheerful and cheap and offered a beach; what more could we want? Secretly, I was wishing for a "safe harbour." After checking in, we were presented with our key. With a bit of dramatic fanfare and a "ta-dah," I opened the door with a flourish to discover pink, floral linoleum staring back at me. It reminded me of my grandmother's upstairs bedroom. I recalled that, when I was a kid, Nana's lino was the identical floral pattern, only in blue.

When Mom and Nana were settled at the kitchen table, chatting over a cup of tea, I used to sneak up the stairs on the pretence that I had to visit the washroom. I'd purposely flush the toilet a couple of times, then tip-toe into Nana's bedroom. I'd sit on the bench with its shiny, wine-coloured, satin seat and admire myself, from flattering angles, in the large dressing-table mirror.

There, in front of me, sat plump powder puffs that were itching to be used. They were situated on top of round boxes of loose powder. I would grab the puffs, dunk them into powder and dab my face. The powder dust floated around me like a halo. After the powdering, my face looked much whiter and creamier than ever before. Next, strong-smelling perfume would find its way behind my ears and between my imaginary breasts, which hopefully would develop into a magnificent bosom in four or five years. Then, I'd fluff up my hair and pin it up with the bobby pins sitting on her dresser. I would primp and preen and become Elizabeth Taylor, the movie star, except I was a mere four foot four, skinny as a rake, and all of eight years of age.

I often wondered why Mom and Nana never mentioned anything about my white, powdery face or the fact that I was reeking of perfume like a bordello babe following my upstairs adventures. They kept my secret. My childhood trip down memory lane was quickly interrupted when Jack motioned me over to sit beside him on the bed.

Now we're talking, I thought to myself. Generally, I try not to be too bold or brazen.

We had been an "item," now for all of five months. That was a record, compared to other guys I had dated, relationships which were measured in seconds and in hours. Even though I have been married twice, I had this knack of repelling rather than attracting men.

"Have a listen to the springs," he said, as he bounced up and down on the bed. We bounced in unison and the entire bed began creaking away along with the bookcase headboard making a thumping and banging noise against the wall. Like an exuberant couple of kids we bounced higher and the creaking and banging grew louder as we laughed and finally toned it down. Jack put his arm around me and drew me close and planted a gentle kiss on my cheek.

"So much for quiet lovemaking tonight," he teased. He had a marvellous, yet gentle, playful way about him.

"I don't care if everyone in the resort hears us," I replied, with conviction, as I kissed him back hard and passionately. Our relationship was blossoming, and this was our first time away together; nothing was going to spoil it.

"Okay, let's change into our bathing suits, and I'll race you to the beach," he said, as he stripped down and put one leg, then the other, into his suit and pulled it up to his waist. I grabbed mine out of the suitcase, jumped into it and tucked a couple of towels under my arm. We flew out the door.

We ran toward the water but had to slow down some, since the pathway leading to the beach was fairly steep. The sand felt warm underfoot. We looked around, and luckily there wasn't a single soul in sight. Sitting down in the wooden lawn chairs, we luxuriated in complete isolation.

"That's the beauty of a September getaway. No bugs either," I added, as I scanned the landscape for dive-bomber mosquitoes.

We could hear a waterfall cascading down the far side of the rock formation. Oh, how I adore the chunky roughness of the Canadian Shield. As we held hands, the silence was broken by the sound of a Sea-Doo engine revving up. The sound appeared to be emanating from a secluded area of the beach further down from us. It became louder; we could see a rider emerging on the water, still at a distance.

Upon closer inspection, I was fascinated to see the Sea-Doo driver circling near our beach. I immediately noticed he was wearing a life jacket and nothing else. His bum crack was clearly visible in the hot afternoon sunshine. I thought, he's going to get his bum sunburned. I bolted up and took a closer look. Jack actually stood up and walked toward the shore for a better view. We giggled and tittered away.

"This isn't exactly the French Riviera, it's Northern Ontario. It's looking more exciting," I exclaimed.

"You betcha, that must be a nude beach," Jack blurted out as he pointed to a spot a few kilometres away. "Where are our binoculars when we need them?"

The Sea-Doo rider didn't circle any closer, although I still had my eyes trained on his backside, and I could sort of make out his facial features. He did have some sense of modesty, after all. Following a few more circling rounds, he disappeared back to the other beach, much to our disappointment.

"I think he was giving us a cheap thrill," Jack mentioned.

We dove into the water to cool off. After an invigorating swim, we dried off and walked back to our "palatial digs." I whipped up some egg salad sandwiches, a trusty summer staple. We sat outside in front of the complex. It was still early in the day, and surprisingly no one else had arrived. We had the place to ourselves. We lazed about in our lawn chairs and read for a while. I had my nose in a novel, and Jack read the paper from end to end.

That night we gave the bed, and ourselves, a work out and made love. No such luxury as a pillow-top mattress was to be found at this rustic resort. The extra sound effects of the springs creaking and groaning beneath us and the headboard banging against the wall didn't deter us one bit. Jack was a fabulous lover. I had to concede that he was good at most everything, although he wasn't perfect, thank God! It was obvious he had been around and involved in many relationships since his divorce. He possessed a natural charm, and I adored his wicked sense of humour. He had a big heart too. That was the trait I found most appealing.

However, I was still holding back some, a little timid about giving the relationship my all. I'd been burned too many times. My relationships all started out like gangbusters and fizzled like a wet firecracker after a few months. Slightly jaded, that best described me, but always willing to give it another go. Lying beside him, after the loving, I decided to forget the odds and shoot for the moon.

"We're fortunate nobody is here yet. We would have caused quite a stir with our love-making on the creaking bed with the noisy headboard rattling away," he said, "and that adjoining door in our room isn't very soundproof either," pointing to the door, which had a rather large, gaping crack all the way around it. There wasn't even any weather stripping tacked to it to muffle sound.

I mentioned, "I'm curious what our neighbours will be like. They could be quiet seniors or rabble-rousing juniors, who knows? Tomorrow, we'll find out as this place will be full of guests, like us, here on the off-season deal."

"You were ever so romantic last night," I said, as I rolled over and snuggled into his arms. Gazing directly into my eyes, he pulled me tighter, giving me the sweetest kiss that barely brushed my cheek. I felt a jolt of warmth passing through me. With his strong arms wrapped around me, I was ensconced in a "safe harbour" where no harm could come to me, for at least tonight.

With the first shaft of morning light filtering through the curtains, I announced, "I have first dibs on the bathroom," as my feet hit the floor.

Breakfast didn't go exactly as planned. The omelette never cooked properly on the hot plate provided. I hadn't cooked on a hot plate for decades; the heat was uneven, at least that was my best excuse. Plus, the milk had separated, since it was an almond brand and lactose-free, a healthy variety. The end result was a limp, watery entrée that didn't look or taste like an omelette. For all I know, I may have created an exotic, new mystery dish. My friends always teased me by saying, "Stick to the bedroom! You're more skilled there than in the kitchen." I think I'll take their advice.

We checked out the lay of the land around the resort. A nice-sized pool and a hot tub that looked like it had been uprooted years ago from the Playboy Mansion in California. I could almost visualize Hugh Hefner and his bevy of girls cavorting about in the water. There were even stringy, fake vines hanging off the makeshift roof. This resort had obviously seen more playful days.

Walking toward the beach, we decided to take the paddle boat out for a spin. Jack suggested that I manoeuvre it. He caught on quickly that I was apprehensive to take the lead in anything, let alone the steering of a boat. Although, this particular model didn't have a high-powered outboard motor—it moved by foot power, and our speed depended on how fast we could pedal.

How hard could it be to steer? I thought to myself. I took my cue and grabbed the stick shift (or whatever that steering mechanism was called), and we pedalled away. As captain, I fearlessly navigated the boat all around the bay. At that point, I was feeling quite confident manoeuvring the rudder. It was exhilarating to skim over the water. We were travelling at a very good clip, pedalling very fast. Cottages of all shapes and sizes were coming into view. We stopped in the middle of the lake to give our feet and legs a rest from the frantic pedalling. We just coasted for a while.

I spotted a lone Canada goose swimming toward us. Jack noticed her, too. "We have company joining us! Quick, open the bag of bread crusts we brought with us, to feed the ducks," he suggested. He took a handful of bread and flung it toward the goose. I also threw crusts over the other side of the boat. The water was soon dotted with pieces of bread. A smaller, brown duck suddenly appeared out of nowhere and gulped down her share. The big goose was scooping up loads of bread, siphoned through her large beak. It appeared she had a voracious appetite.

In no time, we emptied the bag of crusts. We thought our feathered friends would swim away immediately. That's exactly what happened with the brown duck; she was gone in a flash. The goose, however, followed us and wouldn't leave our side. I noticed that she was favouring a wing, which was dragging down slightly lower than the other one, obviously broken. That's probably why she was so hungry. She would experience difficulty gathering food.

"I wish we would have brought more bread," I said. I continually glanced at her swimming around either side of the boat, as we paddled along. I spoke to our water visitor in hushed tones, so as not to scare her. "You are a beautiful goose, the fairest on the bay," I cooed to her. I think Jack thought I was slightly nuts conversing with the goose, but he didn't say a word about it. She was ever so tame and stayed for at least an hour, trailing behind us.

After our goose left, we stopped to give our legs a rest from continuous paddling. The bay was still and calm. We sat quietly and took it all in.

Jack broke our silence. "When I was a teenager, I worked as a camp leader every summer at a lake close by here. I loved it. The kids were fantastic. We swam, taught them some crafts, and we camp leaders wrote and performed in musicals for the kids and parents, for their last night at camp. I still remember the lyrics to one of the songs I wrote for a production."

He proceeded to sing a rousing couple of bars about a young girl becoming interested in boys. He couldn't remember the name of the musical, but he certainly remembered the lively lyrics. He had a pretty good singing voice to boot!

"You're so lucky, I swear that you have horse shoes up your patootie," I told him. "What a fantastic summer job, when you're a kid."

"Yeah it was neat, but you know all those summers spent at camp? I never made any good friends. I did my job and worked with the kids and teased the girls and had fun. But, everyone just sort of ignored me," he said sadly.

"That's too bad," I replied, "Were you shy?"

"Yes, sort of," he admitted and looked away.

Here was a guy who was super-confident and successful. He was a marketing guru and was booked for speaking engagements. I knew I had hit a sensitive area.

"As a teenager I spent a week every summer at a friend's rented cottage," I told him. "There was a roller rink at the lake. Oh, how I loved roller-skating. And when darkness came, we sat around the campfire every night roasting marshmallows, with her family. My friend and I talked constantly about school and of boys that we had crushes on. We were thirteen at the time. When I arrived home, my legs were completely covered by giant, oozing mosquito bites. They took forever to heal. I felt so self-conscious, I didn't wear shorts for the rest of the summer."

Neither one of us wanted to leave this floating sanctuary and continue our paddling. It would never be as perfect as this moment.

Jack was first to break the spell. He let go of my hand, and said, reluctantly, "Come on, we better get a move on, let's pedal our way to our suite."

Back at the resort, people started arriving; it was Saturday afternoon. As we entered our room, a youngish couple, who appeared to be in their late twenties, were just unlocking the suite next door. They literally dumped their suitcases, as we heard the thud on the floor through the adjoining door. That night, the conversation we overheard got really heated.

"You pothead, that's all you are," she yelled at the top of her lungs. "Can't you stay sober for one bloody night? I don't know why we're still together!"

He angrily retorted, "No one else would put up with you, you horrible bitch."

"This is my holiday too, why did you have to spoil it by getting stoned?" she screeched at him and then broke down into a sob. Her sobbing got louder.

"Ah, shut up; don't bring on the tears, you'll get no sympathy from me. You're always on my case, you never let up," he yelled.

We just sat silently on the couch, holding hands, not wanting to talk or have them know that their fight was being overheard. Later on, the language got really foul. The commotion finally stopped with the slamming of the door. One of them had left in a fit of anger. It was 1:30 in the morning, and we could finally go to bed and get some sleep. When I climbed into bed next to Jack, I secretly hoped that our relationship would never drop to that level of ugliness. I hated confrontation and scenes like that one we had just overheard.

In the morning we decided to enjoy the playboy mansion hot tub, complete with the tacky vines. I half expected starlet Pamela Anderson to waltz into the tub at any moment. It sure had star power! The tub was deserted, as was the pool. We jumped in and managed to get the jets working full blast. Soon, we had company. The resort owner asked, "Do you folks mind if I join you? I like to be nude in the hot tub!"

"No, problem," I said, without skipping a beat, as though this was an everyday occurrence. Jack nodded that it was okay by him. He winked at me just as the owner folded his long legs over the side of the tub and sat down. He was a man I believed to be in his early forties and very good looking. Thankfully, I still had my glasses on, but I didn't know where to look. My glance was immediately aimed lower, from the neck down, in the water, not focused on his face. I had a bird's eye view of the resort owner's taut, naked body. Glory be, what a thrill to behold! His thick penis was floating in the water like a bob-o-link, rising and falling with the motion of the jets. His son, muscular and maybe about eighteen, also arrived on the scene. I discreetly checked over the side of the hot tub to determine if he was wearing a bathing suit. He climbed into the tub. I thought for a moment we hit pay dirt and would have a nude father and son team. I looked over at Jack, and he was grinning away. Alas, damn it all, the younger version was wearing a bathing suit. Now, as a cardinal rule, whenever I'm hot tubbing, no matter if my glasses get hopelessly splashed or fogged up from the jet spray, I'll always wear them.

I had to throw out the bathing suit I was wearing that day in the hot tub, as the chemicals in the water must have been slightly out of whack. They totally bleached my multi-coloured suit, so that it was unrecognizable. The same thing happened to Jack's suit. However, we agreed, the experience was well worth the price of a couple of new bathing suits.

This was our swan song at the Last Chance resort, or whatever it was called. There was a full harvest moon and everything else around us was inky black. The crickets were serenading us with a concert of melodious chirping. We sat outside at midnight searching the sky for the Big Dipper. I found it first, and then Jack pointed to Orion. I'm convinced that the stars and constellations were all aligned for us. We were in total sync with each other, without saying much. Holding hands made everything right with the world.

We went inside and threw back the covers and made love like it meant something. I didn't want to leave the peace and serenity of his arms. Oh, how I treasured my time with him in the "safe harbour." In the morning, we packed up our gear and headed back to Toronto. We were quiet for most of the drive home. We both knew the magic we experienced was going to be hard to duplicate when we went back to our separate lives in the city.

A year has passed since our visit to the Last Chance resort. Snow is falling; it's the coldest winter on record. I'm thinking summer thoughts about the Canada goose with the broken wing who followed us behind the paddle boat. I was aware of the code of the wild. A goose that is injured will experience extreme difficulty. Others of the same species aren't friendly and will pick on her or even kill her. When a bird or goose is injured, it's considered weak. That's why she was alone, not wishing to attract the attention of other geese. I wondered if she survived the winter by herself, in her habitat, nursing her broken wing.

I shared some common ground with that goose. My heart was broken when Jack and I split up for good, after a year together. I figure the goose and I are both seeking a new "safe harbour." Although she is probably a much younger bird, as I celebrate my sixty-ninth birthday next month. I'm convinced that both of us will find our "safe harbour" somewhere in our travels. In the meantime, dear reader, keep me in mind if you know of a great guy out there, someone who doesn't mind soggy omelettes—I'm still looking.

IS ROMANCE DEAD OR JUST HALF DEAD?

He said, sweetly, “Do come up to my room.”
I was twenty: “Right away, I’m over the moon.”

I was thirty: “Once the kids are asleep.”
“Forget it; you’ll be too tired to leap.”

At seventy-five: “How about a great big kiss?”
“Okay, I might keel over for a moment’s bliss.”

At eighty-five: “I’ll take out my teeth, before I pucker up.”
“I prefer seeing your teeth in, not in a cup.”

At ninety-eight: “In the mood to make whoopee, come to me.”
“I’m a-coming; just let me hoist up my good knee.”

***Mary Ellen Koroscil** was born and raised in Moose Jaw, Saskatchewan and this Western community has produced an amazing source of writing material for her to draw upon. Although, as a publicist she has operated her own public relations business for many years, she is dividing her time on various other styles of writing, rather than focusing solely on writing press releases. Writing poetry and short stories appears to be where her passion lies. She still loves working with authors, helping them to create the ‘buzz,’ in the media and she also promotes singers/songwriters and entertainers. Co-chairing the Courtneypark Literary Circle for several years has been a terrific experience for her. This wonderful group helps to inspire her to grow as a writer.*

Konrad Brinck

JOY AND HAPPINESS

The big day had arrived! After years of trying to become parents, after being told that the chances of Jackie becoming pregnant were remote and after nine months of waiting for Children's Aid to find a newborn baby for us, the day had arrived.

It was two months earlier when our social worker called us and told us that there was a young girl in Nova Scotia who was pregnant and had decided to give up her baby for adoption. She was only 17 years old and felt it was best to find good parents for her baby and give her or him a chance at a bright and promising future.

The father of the baby was a schoolmate of hers and had agreed with her decision. Now our waiting game started.

We used the time to get the nursery ready. Everything was decorated in yellow. We didn't know if we would have a boy or a girl. The basement was filled with boxes of diapers of every size. The closet was filled with baby clothes, towels, sheets, wipes, wraps, bottles and everything a baby could need. There were stuffed animals and baby toys everywhere.

We were ready! We had agreed to adopt the baby no matter what, boy or girl, poor health, birth defect or any other handicap. We wanted it to be as realistic a parenting experience as possible and with that there are no guarantees or choices. You take what fate will give you.

We were not going to turn another child away. It broke our hearts when we had to do it the first time. Even though we had specified that we wanted a newborn, no other conditions attached, Children's Aid contacted us after three months to tell us that they might have a child for us. When the social worker came to our home she told us that this child was not exactly what we wanted but she was going to let us decide. She showed us a picture of Elizabeth, an eighteen-month-old toddler. She already talked, walked and was long past the infant stage Jackie and I wanted to be part of.

We gave it a lot of thought and felt like lesser human beings for rejecting Elizabeth. We were assured that there was no problem placing her with another family, but that feeling of denying a young child your love and a home was one of the toughest decisions we have ever made, and we did not want to have to make that choice again.

This time we were going to accept a newborn without any conditions.

August 12th. The long awaited call from the social worker came: "It's a healthy baby girl!"

Our excitement and anxiety grew. The only thing in our way now was the legal 30-day waiting period after the date of birth, during which the mother could still change her mind about giving her baby up for adoption. That thirty days of nail-biting was filled with frequent reports from the social worker on how our little girl was progressing.

September 12th. Our little baby had officially become a ward of the Crown and we were now able to go and get her.

September 13th. We purchased our return tickets to Halifax to pick up our daughter the next day. Our anxiety and anticipation was torturing us. We had a sleepless night.

September 14th. We arrived in Halifax on the first plane from Toronto. It was a bright and sunny morning. The social worker was waiting at the airport to take us to her office to have all the papers signed. During the short drive to her office she talked about the background of the parents and how difficult it was for the mother to make the right decision. She told us that our baby was the cutest baby she had ever seen.

When we arrived at the Children's Aid offices we completed the necessary paperwork and noticed that the birth mother had named the baby Tasha Joy. We were upset. We had already decided to name her Toni Belinda and asked if we could rename her. We were assured there was no problem and the final adoption papers and her birth certificate would read Toni Belinda Brinck. What a relief!

After the formalities were completed, we had to wait for the foster mother to arrive with our little girl. We were told that there would be a slight delay and we should go for lunch and return in an hour. We had no appetite and a short walk around downtown Halifax was not very relaxing at all.

Time was crawling. Why was there a delay? We were getting more anxious by the minute. We returned early and were told it would be another thirty minutes. The explanation was that the Doctor, who was to perform a last check-up to make sure our little girl was in good health, was delayed. It was Saturday and his practice was closed. He had to be called in from his home to go to the foster mother's home to do the examination.

I kept looking at my watch nervously. We felt like time was standing still. Was it hot or were my nerves making me perspire? We paced back and forth in the large boardroom. It had a large table and comfortable looking leather armchairs, but who could sit still at a time like this? Once in a while we stopped our pacing and looked out the windows that were wide open on this warm September day. The street was deserted.

Finally, we saw a taxi pull up to the front door and a woman emerged holding a baby wrapped in a blanket.

Our hearts were beating so hard that I thought they could be heard echoing through the hallways of the building. The door opened and the foster mother entered the room and put the little bundle into my wife's arms and said: "Here is your new baby daughter." With that, she and the social worker left the room.

Jackie and I looked at this cute little baby. She was fast asleep. Suddenly we both started crying uncontrollably. Tears of joy ran down our cheeks. We smiled at each other, unable to speak. No words were necessary to express our feelings of complete joy. Jackie kissed our daughter lovingly on the forehead while I was wiping the tears off of our faces. The baby was totally unaware that she had just been put into the arms of her new parents.

She looked like an angel, dressed in a lacy white dress with a matching cap. A lock of her hair peeked out from under her cap and curled across her forehead. One of our tears that fell on her cheek woke her up. When she saw us she started crying along with us.

There we were, together as a family for the first time, crying away.

I could not remember a time in my life when I was laughing and crying at the same time. Nothing could have prepared me for that moment.

The emotions I felt, when I laid eyes on her for the first time and when I held her in my arms, cannot be expressed in words. Tears still well up inside of me today when I talk about that moment. I was emotionally drained, exhausted but filled with such bliss when I finally calmed down.

The social worker gave us half an hour together before she poked her head into the room and asked if we were ready to go to the airport. We had regained our composure and were anxious to get home.

Once at home, Toni was not a happy baby. She wouldn't stop crying for the next three weeks, unless she had a soother in her mouth, was eating or asleep. We never found out why she cried so much during that time. Jackie and I were desperately looking for answers. Was she aware of turmoil in her first four weeks of life? Was that why she had trouble settling down? Or was she just testing us?

If it was a test we must have passed it because after the crying stopped, we became a loving, caring and happy family.

The Penis Trilogy

Most men, when talking about their penis, will talk about their virility, conquests, performance, size and glory.

I believe that there are many more tales to tell about their failures, embarrassments and painful memories.

Here are three stories of the more 'painful' sort.

1. The Unwanted Erection

In 1966, I was diagnosed with high blood-pressure and my doctor thought it was necessary to have me checked out at the local hospital. One of the tests was a cystoscopy, which in those days meant a short stay in the hospital to recover from the procedure.

For those of you who don't know what a cystoscopy is, I will explain.

A cystoscope is a rigid instrument about 30 centimetres long and has the thickness of my little finger. This instrument is inserted into the opening of the penis and shoved through the urethra all the way up to the bladder.

This description should make you cringe, and your assumption that this is painful is absolutely correct.

Normally, patients will get a local anaesthetic to dull the pain. However, back in Germany I assume that half the doctors believed the pain was bearable and the others must have been trained by Dr. Mengele or were disciples of the Marquis de Sade.

No anaesthetic was provided.

When told to disrobe, lie down on the examination table and cover myself with the sheet that the good-looking nurse handed me, I did so without hesitation.

I had overlooked the slit, strategically located in the centre of the sheet and even if I had seen it and knew what it was for, I would still not have been inclined to expose my genitals anyway. When the doctor, also a female, came into the examination room she noticed that I had not laid bare the part of my body that she was most interested in for purely medical reasons.

At the age of nineteen it didn't take much to get an erection, especially not if a female reaches under a sheet to pull out your manhood and exhibits it to a gorgeous young nurse that is observing the action with great interest.

It must have taken less than a millisecond for my little soldier to rise to the occasion and stand at full attention.

The doctor looked at my now fully erect penis. She nonchalantly grabbed it with her left hand, leaving the head exposed, and smacked it with her right hand like the bottom of a ketchup bottle, mumbling "We can't have that here now, can we?"

I sat straight up, emitting a short yelp of pain, knocked my head on the overhead light, and then fell back onto the table, wanting to die of shame and embarrassment.

I don't know what hurt more, the physical pain of the smack to my little friend, the insertion of the cystoscope or the humiliation of this whole episode.

2. No Toy for a Pussy

The party at the Leschs' was over and it was time for us to go home on a beautiful summer night. My convertible was parked in their driveway with the roof down and I didn't bother to check the backseat before driving home.

Only after we got home when I was closing the roof that Jackie noticed the little kitten all snuggled up on my jacket in the back seat. We decided to keep her for the night and call Merle in the morning to let her know that her little kitten had deserted her and we had granted her temporary asylum.

Jackie put a few pillows down for her to sleep, but the kitty decided to cuddle up with us on our bed.

At this point I should maybe mention that I sleep in the nude, especially on hot summer nights. I prefer fresh air caressing my naked body to closed windows and an air-conditioned bedroom. I assume everybody is aware that men quite frequently have an involuntary early morning erection, also known as a 'woody.'

That morning, the sun must have just come up; the cat woke up and found herself in a strange bed without any toys. She was probably looking for something to play with. It must have been precisely at that moment that she noticed something moving lower down on the bed, below my belly and seemingly sprouting out from between my legs.

I can just picture her slowly crawling towards this mysterious mushroom-shaped object growing and swaying back and forth with every deep snore. Maybe she thought it was an inflatable toy or even a scratching post put there for her amusement.

It doesn't really matter what she thought; her instincts told her to pounce on it and try to scratch and bite it into submission.

And that is exactly what she did!

The pain was excruciating as I got jolted out of my deep sleep and tried to remove whatever was attacking and mauling my penis.

Not expecting my violent reaction, the cat sunk her claws even deeper into my rapidly shrinking member, but my earth-shattering screaming finally convinced her to let go of my most sensitive body part. She jumped off the bed, partially assisted by my throwing motion, and ran for dear life.

Jackie snapped out of her deep sleep seeing the cat flying through the room and me holding onto my scrotum and screaming in pain.

After she had examined the damage, she started laughing uncontrollably, making jokes about me having been attacked by a scratching and biting pussy.

I eventually rediscovered my sense of humour and told the story to Reggie and Merle upon returning their cat. Jackie wouldn't have allowed me to keep this little episode a secret from her friends anyway.

Happily, my penis and I suffered no permanent damage, but for some reason the cat never trusted me nor came close to me again.

I wonder why?

3. The Sperm Test

My penis and I, as well as Jackie, had a fun and exciting time in our many attempts to produce an offspring. However, it became increasingly obvious after many months that our efforts were not producing the wanted results.

Jackie's gynaecologist, wanting to eliminate the obvious reasons, suggested I should have a sperm test performed at the local hospital. He handed me the requisition and told me that no appointment was necessary.

When I arrived at the reception desk of Peel Memorial Hospital, there were a few people in the waiting area. So that nobody could hear me, I quietly whispered to the receptionist that I was referred by my doctor for some tests.

Bad choice of words.

She looked at the requisition and in a loud, boisterous voice announced for everybody to hear: "Your doctor is a gynaecologist?"

I felt everybody looking at me and before I could correct her she said in an even louder voice, "I see, you are here for a sperm count."

Now I could definitely feel the stares of the people in the waiting area. I felt myself blushing furiously as I was told to take a seat and wait.

A few minutes later she called me to her desk, handed me a sample vial and an instruction sheet on how to proceed. I didn't think I needed instructions on how to clean my penis and masturbate into a jar.

Her next move stunned me.

She called a young volunteer, a candy striper as they were called in those days, and told her to take me to a washroom and wait there until I was done and then to take the vial straight to the lab. Apparently time is of the essence since sperm has a high mortality rate.

Unfortunately, I had not thought of bringing a Playboy or any other gentleman's magazine with me to help get me aroused and knowing that a teenage female volunteer, who knew what I was doing, was standing on the other side of the door was not exactly putting me in the right frame of mind to complete the task at hand.

Finally, after some vigorous manual labour, my little willie started growing in the palm of my hand. Precisely at that moment I heard footsteps coming my way and a voice saying to the volunteer; "Why are you standing around here, don't you have anything to do?"

"I'm supposed to wait for this guy to finish his sperm test and then take the jar right away to the lab for analysis," she replied. The snickering and snarky remark that followed caused my little friend to deflate and that meant I had to start all over again.

After an assertive effort, when I thought I was close, I heard footsteps approaching once again.

The voice said, "You mean to tell me he's still at it?"

There wasn't another word said, just snickering and giggling as the footsteps faded away.

My willie had again opted for a full retreat and I was ready to concede defeat.

The thought of having to explain to a teenager why the jar was not filled motivated me to one more final herculean effort.

Just before my arm fell off and my hand cramped up, I reached my goal of releasing millions of little tadpoles into the jar.

After checking in the mirror to see if I had popped a vein during this strenuous exercise, I wiped the perspiration off of my face, opened the door and handed the jar to the young lady, avoiding any eye contact. As I left the hospital, I still felt like everybody was staring at me.

As for the time I took to complete the test, I'm sure there is a medical note somewhere in my file stating that premature ejaculation is not one of my problems.

Konrad Brinck *was born in Berlin, Germany, in 1946 and immigrated to Canada in 1968. He started writing his memoirs in 2012 after a long career in sales and marketing. He is known as a good story teller, but so far he has been limited to writing for special interest and ethnic German magazines. He is presently a member in various writers groups and has taken courses and workshops to learn more about the art of writing. Konrad is happily married and has one daughter and two lovely granddaughters.*

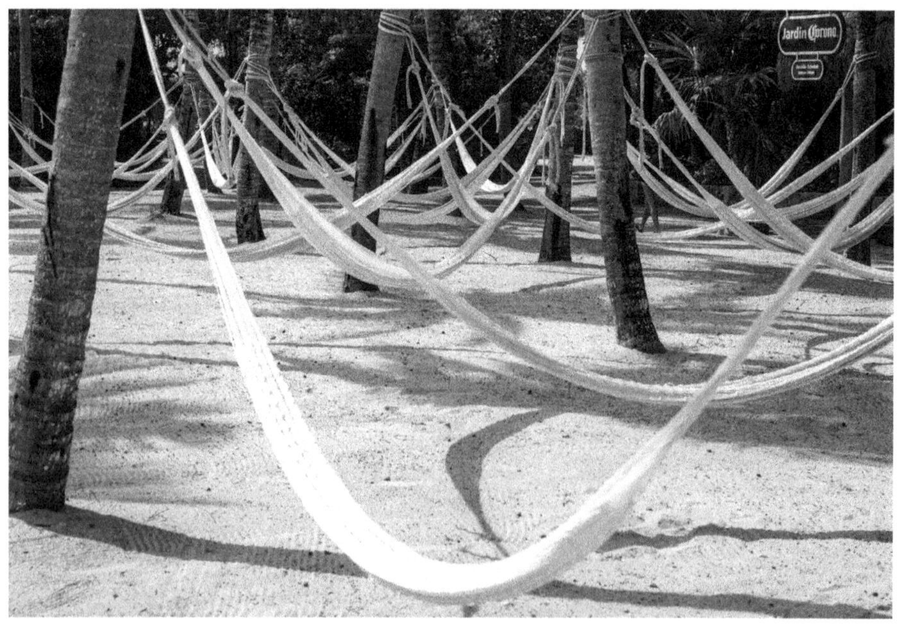

'Hammocks' by Ash Anthony Xavier

Carmela Zita Kapeleris

IF LIFE IS SO SHORT

If life is so short,
why do we DO so many things we DON'T LIKE,
and like so many things we DON'T DO?
Why do we worry about DOING things right,
instead of just doing the RIGHT things?
Are you doing what you BELIEVE IN,
or are you settling for what everyone else is doing?
Tell me, which is worse: failing or never trying…
If we learn from our mistakes,
why are we always so afraid to make them?
What would you do differently
if you knew nobody would JUDGE YOU?

In five years from now,
will you remember what you did yesterday…
What you did the day before that…
Or the day before that?
Do you feel like you've lived this day a hundred times before?
Do you feel the difference
between being alive and TRULY LIVING?
When was the last time you noticed
the sound of your own breathing?
And when it's all said and done…
will you have SAID MORE than you've DONE?

INVISIBLE

(Dedicated to my son Chris who inspired me to write)

See me
I am Invisible
I am the Wind
Feel me
Soothing your soul
And your skin

Your soul
Is like the Wind
The wind
Is your soul

The birds fly
They soar
They land
They float with the Wind

They are free
They have no boundaries
I hear them
They are not INVISIBLE

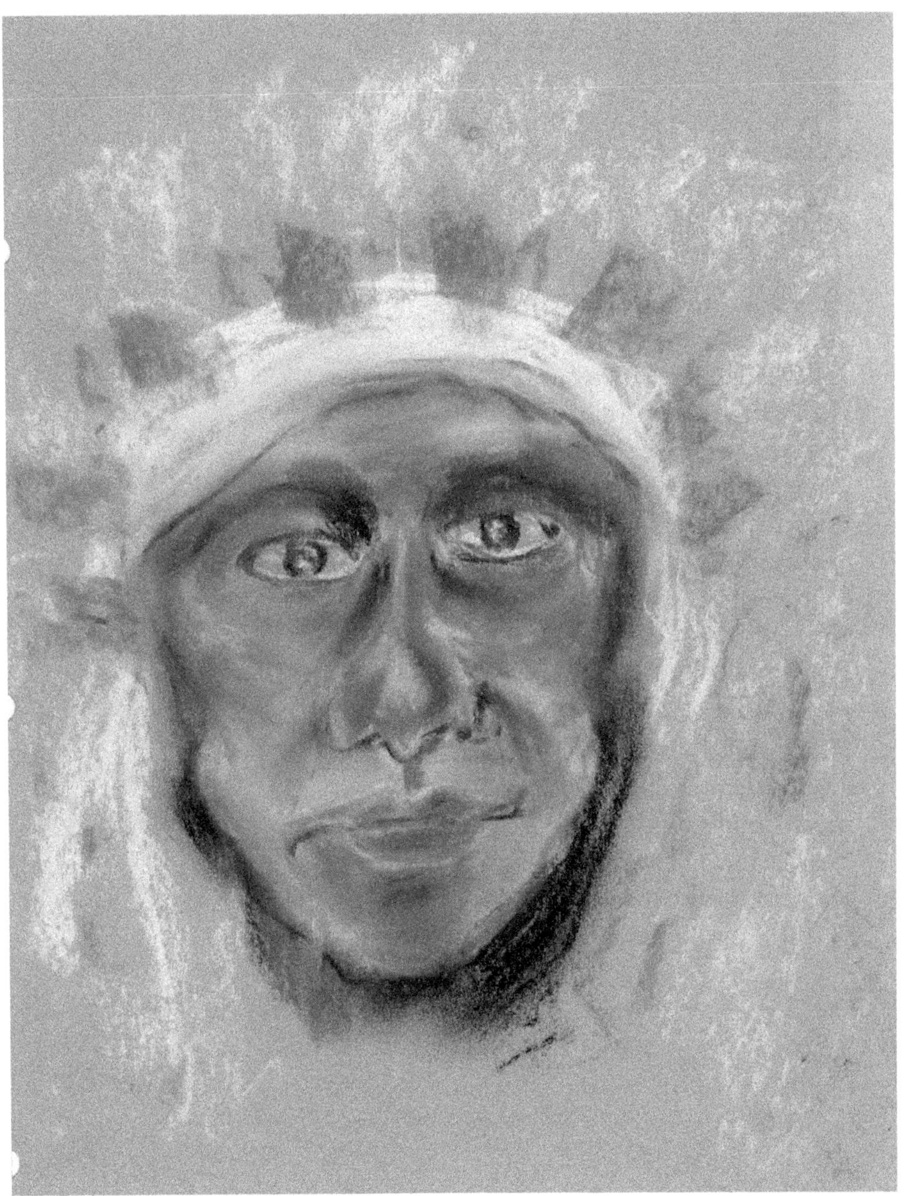

'Indian' by Carmela Zita-Kapeleris

THE GREATEST POWER ON EARTH

Love is the greatest power on earth
It conquers all things
Your soul soars high
While your spirit sings

It conquers the birds and bees
The mountains and the trees
The mind and the body
The heart and the soul
A power so great
Beyond your control
As love grows in you
Beauty grows too
For love is beauty of the soul
And it radiates within you
The world is but a canvas
To our imagination
The truth is living and loving
Every situation
Everything is possible
For the person that believes
The greatest miracle is love
Says the blind man who sees

Destiny is not a matter of chance
It is a matter of choice
People spread the word
Dance and rejoice

It is more than enough
If the only prayer you say in life
Is thank you for love
And thank you for my life

VOLCANO

Night falls upon us
Like a warm shadowy blanket
Covering and protecting us
Like a shield of shiny metal

Filling us with promise
And fantasies of the days to come

Praying and hoping
To mask the hurt and the pain

Embedded
Encrusted
Deep below the surface

Like a VOLCANO
Ready to erupt
Hot Scorching deathly lava

Anxious to spread its fury
Over the land
A roar that strikes fear
In all who hear

Destruction of nature
In its path of glory
That runs deep through all its beauty
But Never being SORRY

without a thought
without a reason
without remorse

Earth could stand the pressure no more

Clinging, twisting, turning
To find the proper solutions
Reciting the forms
That come in many illusions

Chanting, Raving,
Chemicals of all kinds
Intricately woven in a template
To soothe the human mind

Telling tales in a sequence
Of unmistakable truths
Driving depression
Into every enchanted story

To pacify and numb the sensation
Of the blissful sublime
Like an Iceberg
Frozen in space and time

Waiting to be soothed
With the rays of energy that shine

Hoping to be thawed
With a gentle caress

Longing to be unbound
And cleansed
In anticipation of starting Anew

Hard as a rock
Cold as ice
Sharp as glass
Cuts like a knife

Like the Cravings in an old Oak tree
That once had symbols of you and me

Two hearts intertwined
One yours and one mine

And through it all
It weathered the storm
And stood the test of time

NEW YORK! NEW YORK!

New York, New York
The city that never sleeps
To enjoy with friends you love
And make memories run deep

New York, New York
Spacious and grand
A city so large and diverse
It gives culture to every land

New York, New York
People come from far and wide
To experience the energy of a city
With so much power and pride

New York, New York
Precious lady with the torch
Standing tall
Only to witness
In the midst of the early morning
Two towers fall

New York, New York
We marvel at your magnificence
Every landmark, every bridge
Every person, every sound

Humility, tolerance
Hurt and screaming
Pain and tragedy
Rebirth and victory

New York! New York!
So proud of your perseverance
So grateful for your existence

RED VELVET, RED ROSE

(Dedicated to the two Roses in my life)

We plant the seed
We nurture the soil
We water the earth
We watch the buds grow

Energy from the sun
Oxygen from the air
Beauty is everywhere

The sensual aroma
Of nature so pure
A blossoming creature
With all its allure

We cherish it
We adore it
We revel in its glory

Every petal, every leaf
Every thorn
Tells its own story

Red velvet petals
Longing to stay
Drifting down to the ground
Day by day

The beauty is gone
The memory lives on
Don't cut me away

Leave me
Love me
Care for me
My rose will blossom another day

JOY!

Open your heart, Open you mind,
Leave the memories of your past far behind

You can sing, you can dance
You can achieve your own glory
You can love, be loved, laugh
Breathe and be full of joy

Every day is new
Every day is a discovery
Every day is a loving journey

Open your heart, open your mind
Everyone join together
Release the boundaries
That bind
The spiritual connection
To the mind

Feel the energy
Feel the emotions

Feel my strength
Feel my love
Look up at the soft clouds and see me
Soaring free as a dove

Look into the river and see me
Drifting into the magic of the unknown
Enjoying every minute as I relish and roam

Look at the trees, so luscious and green
The most beautiful vision that I've ever seen

Smell the air, Feel the sun
Majestic mountains, rivers that run

Roaring valley, soaring hills
Adventure awaits us with mystical thrills

A new beginning, a fresh start,
I feel this place already nestled deep in my heart

I took the chance
I took the steps
I achieved my goal
I feel so blessed
I feel so loved
This is all for me
I feel JOY!

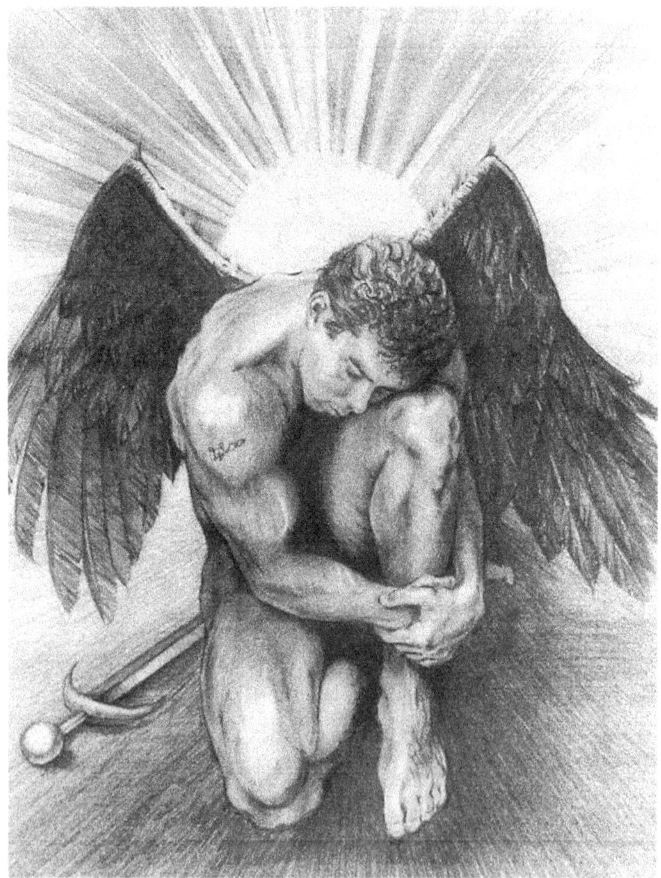

Illustration by Carmela Zita Kapeleris

SILENCE

Silence streams like a welcoming pillow
Nurturing and comforting me in my stillness
An aura of whiteness and light surrounds me
The sweetness of my breath rises through my spirit
Warmth and love is everywhere…

A calm soothes my wandering mind
As the world stops turning, sounds disappear
If only for a minute…

The pounding of my pulse guides me
Like the rhythm of a soft drum
The taste of the air lingers on my tongue
The breeze still fresh on my face

Fire burns in my immortal being
Passion awakens my blissful heart
Living each moment in joy and contentment

The stars from within shine brighter than bright
Rising higher from an inner realm of tranquility
Where awareness of self
The discovery of higher truths
The true nature of reality
And consciousness of mind and body become one
Liberated, gratified and free

Discovering the pure essence of being
Honouring the inner path of harmony
Transcending with love
The journey to the Divine

Beauty and Nature surrounds us
Calm and peace enrapture us
Silence streams through us
Warmth and love is everywhere…

FAMILIAR STRANGER

Your face is familiar
Your voice seems strange

Darkness has fallen
When the sun has risen high

The clouds have passed
But the storm is still there

Your eyes are dark as coal
Your heart is cold as stone

I breathe, I speak
But the words make no sound

Your face is familiar
But your shadow has changed

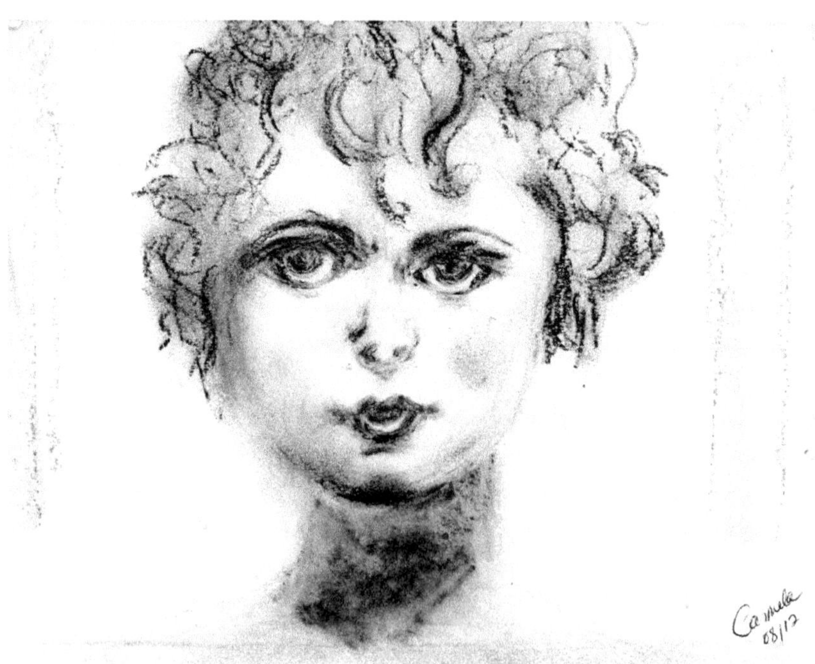

Illustration by Carmela Zita Kapeleris

LITTLE CHILD

Little Child… why do you remember it that way
Wish I could go back and take all that hurt away
My heart bleeds
I can't breathe
I never meant it to be that way

All the time that passed
I had no idea
I showed you my love
I felt it was real
I thought you loved me the way I loved you
I wish with all my heart and pray this is true

I wish I could go back in time and tell that little child,
Not to be scared
Not to be afraid,
It wasn't meant to be that way
You are loved
You are special
You are important and we are here

But our love was so strong
That it came across wrong

Now I wish I had been better
I wish I would have known what to do,
The fact was
That I was just a little child too

Then that little child grew
And became just like you
Now the cycle begins anew
Hope you love that little child too

WHISPERS

Whispers are like chatter
Taking a life of their own
Filling the entity of time
Pretending to be real
In the Whisperer's mind

Whispers are not real
They do not exist
Fabricated by thoughts
That flitter in the foggy
Cloudy murky mist

Slowly and softly they dissipate
Dissolving into the vastness of the universe

For they are only whispers
That disappear with time
Imaginary figments
Of the human mind

Carmela Zita-Kapeleris *was born in Canada to Italian immigrant parents and married into a family with a strong Greek heritage. She has two adult children, both of whom encouraged her to pursue her writing and artistic talents professionally. An avid reader, writer and artist since early childhood with a degree in marketing and business, Carmela also has a passion for helping people find their dream home and has enjoyed a very successful 26 year career in real estate and has been honoured as a Top Business Woman Entrepreneur by a women's organization. She recently began publishing a literary and business newspaper in Mississauga. Some of her most soul-satisfying achievements have been through humanitarian work with organizations such as World Vision Canada, Adopt-a-Senior, Children's Miracle Network, BPW Canada, Stop Child Labour—(nochildisforsale.ca) and founder of 'Women helping Women,' an empowering group. Some of Carmela's writing can be found on her website blog at kapeleris.com/blog/*

Sudha Naimpally

FRIENDSHIP

Friendship is like a mutual promise
That allows you peace.
A pat, a smile or just a friendly squeeze
Puts your mind at ease.
Friendship is like a warm sunray
That never will betray
The confidence, that the deepest secrets
Will be guarded nevertheless.
The unspoken, mutual bond of friends
To stand by, in any circumstance
Just knowing someone is there,
Always for you, one who cares.
A shoulder to cry on,
Firm assurances to rely on,
Encouraging words to succeed on,
Who, but a friend, can you count on?

MOTHER NATURE

The morning dew dampens the face,
Cool breezes soothe with a caress.
The winter sun warms the heart,
White snowflakes, fluffy and light.
The wet sand cools the soles.
Whispering willows, the wind blows,
Wisps of grass dancing in the air,
The bubbling brook rushing without care,
Sticks and stones laced with moss,
Reflections of banks and trees
These are the gifts for nurturing
Abundant for the taking.
Walking in the woods,
Leaves crushing underfoot
Starry nights, feast for the eyes
Thoughts of one's beloved ever on the mind
Such little pleasures that can still Time
Thank you, for your gifts, Mother Nature
Always healing and protecting, past and future.

ONENESS

The spirit that flows,
Through Bosnia and Chechnya
Rwanda and Uganda
In war and peace
Into holocaust and slavery
For eternities
Imbued in sorrow and ecstasy;
All through sensory experiences.
In opposites and similars,
Through inert and living
Mountains and rivers
The enlivening forces
From a ripple or a wisp of grass
To the warm breath,
Give dimension to time and space.
In frost and sunshine
Floods and famines
Gales and hurricanes
In changes and in stillness
That which binds
And winds through veins
From me to a little speck of dust to a nebula
Without exception
Makes everything one and only one
Without the other.

UNSEEN CREATOR

I see the hands of an unseen painter
At dawn and dusk and in between.
Colours galore on the easel of sky
With ever-changing hues.
Silhouettes of birds
Soar over the clouds and things divine,
The Milky Way, stardust and the likes.
The sign of a creator
Of known and unknown,
Bringing to light rivers, mountains,
Forests and transitions of seasons
Shedding light on life's purpose.
His hands are seen all day, every day.
Those who see it, recognize it
And those who don't, in time, may get it.

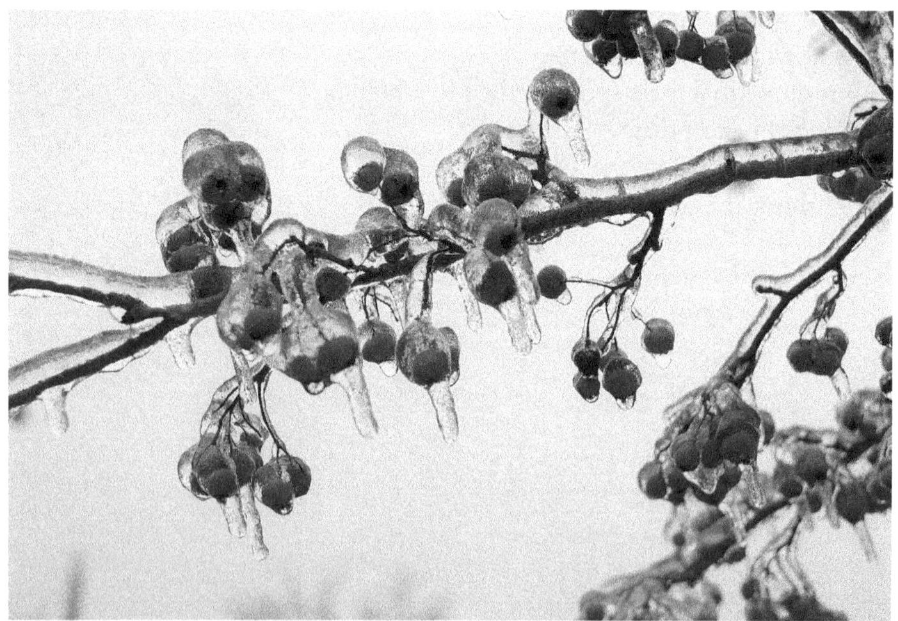

Photograph by Merridy Cox

Tasnim Jivaji

CAN WE DEPART FOR A SECOND?

Can we depart for a second here
from being a people behind a country
and break away from the pack we hide in
pry ourselves from our ghettos and houses of God
leave that flag on the pole and anthem in the wind
and become a person standing alone
a step away from the noisy crowd—quietly alone?

So, when the crowd sways—can you please not
And when it decides—please don't.
And when they chant—hold your breath.
Just for one moment—be still
by yourself be alone an atom
an independent thought
in a world of your own
perfectly still and completely alone.

What do you see, feel, and sense
about the state of affairs in your world?
Where men and women you do not even know
have led you and your future generations?
Why is there so much back-biting and bickering
in the source of your view?
By now we could have created and renamed Earth Euphoria,
for all of you.

Yes, your little personal battles overwhelm you,
and a fight this large in another place so far away
in a language and dress and creed so tarnished
doesn't register as one you must engage in, does it?
But you join in, just to hear or read or grumble or remark upon
and in your charade, they call it 'News' and you,
you miss the world of war

When you have shed your ounce of flesh
and see that it does indeed spill your own blood
Then you learn to comprehend front page lies
and the things which are not said.
And when the book comes, you bother to read
and you know already about the greed
and watch it when it becomes a movie
and you finally see the face of the cheats in reality
gasping because you know where you were then,
when these people were thrown to the lions.

You see today, when suffering prevails;
When suffering prevails in all little places
hangs in the air, commonplace, like
in dramas on TV, making 'rich-people' problems
and crying normal even for small idiotic things
When bullying begins with school
before you can even learn to read and write or meet your Self
One doesn't see the fault meander in, a tiny trickle
drop by drop, seeping in, soaking in, sinking in
to make you question, why? Excuse me—why?

So in the love of life, in the bigger picture, the crowd will see and know
that to submit is peace
or maybe it elevates one high enough
to be able to move from one moment to the next
and in the end (whatever that is) is so diminished
and life goes on as time does fly
and it slips into the past
out of sight dust to dust   out of context
and you are aged now and all that happened
to an old person is a mystery, even to yourself.

P. J. Kapllani

A HOSPITAL FOR HORSES

Daniel Shkurti was a journalist, who was working for the government when he started to think seriously about his accommodation. He had lived for a long time in an old building, which had been used as a hospital for horses before the Second World War.

While nailed to his marital bed, Daniel felt the dampness of the room and a bitter taste in his mouth. He felt that he had been transformed into a sick horse, lingering in that bed, suffering from rheumatism, crushed under the heavy air, smelling like wet dung. He found shelter in that building, after his attempts to occupy another place to live in went in vain. He thought he looked like an old jade with long, skinny legs, a big jaw and long black mane flowing every time he ran against the wind. Perhaps he should have hooves, a harness, a bit and saddle one day.

Daniel was obsessed with the history of this old building that was covered with a reedy roof. As soon as he finished work in his office, he went through some old faded documents that he had found in a battered suitcase, covered by years of dust. He used to get lost in that daily search, while eating green tomatoes sprinkled with a little oil and salt. He imagined going through dozens of medical records and files, where the names of those poor animals had been written. He was surprised about the medications that were used to cure those animals, the doses, the injections and the receipts. He found the addresses of different hospitals, slaughter houses, butcheries and meat factories in Albania and Italy.

The notes which were written in Italian were neat and well-organized in fine handwriting. The files were filled with observations of the course of the illness of these mysterious patients. He was so engrossed in these notes that he forgot that the hours, days, weeks and months were going by quickly. His crazy obsession drove him to take an intensive course in the Italian language. This would be easy and he wouldn't have any obstacles, unlike Graham Greene, when he tried to learn that language.

He heard the distant trot of horses that seemed as if it were approaching the window, during the dark nights. Scared to death, he stared at the ceiling desperately, hoping to escape these thoughts. The strange, contours and shapes like curved backs of horses seemed to be dancing and jumping across the ceiling, which seemed about to collapse on his head.

The horses galloped all night long until dawn. He was terrified at the thought that his body smelled like a horse. Feeling hopeless, he opened the window and all of a sudden he was confronted by a big white snout and flaring nostrils.

Time after time, it seemed to him that he heard horses' neighing in the distance. Huge herds of horses filled his dreams, running with a thundering of hooves across the endless horizon. His dreams followed a pattern that of watching these friendly and devoted animals, which started to bother him, for fear of changing into a bizarre hybrid of horse and man was growing in his mind. He felt bandaged by the white sheets and totally unprotected from imaginary injections. Daniel had an awful feeling of being an ex-patient. He couldn't even eat his favorite food anymore, including meat, eggs, feta cheese and butter. He didn't really care too much about stew. His habits of eating had changed. Now he started to eat salad, cabbage, canned olives, onions, pickles and raw potatoes. He was becoming a vegetarian.

Daniel was trying to find a reasonable solution for himself. This situation wasn't created just because of the history of the environment, where he lived. He was waiting anxiously to see if his skin would be transformed, if hooves were to appear, if his ears grew longer, or if his face began to resemble the shape of a snout, his eyes become enlarged and chest and belly widen. Thank God nothing happened. His skin and face didn't change. Neither did his belly nor his chest. None of these physical changes took place which would have explained the change towards animalism he felt happening deep in his consciousness. He wasn't afraid of people anymore, neither were they afraid of him. The psycho-physiologic disorder was invisible and the most terrible part of this abstraction was taking place in his brain. Daniel couldn't keep his mind off it. He felt the suffering and illness of all those sick horses that had lived in these stalls, which had been built by Italy in 1937. These stalls hadn't changed for a long time, despite the attempts of different regimes to restore them.

He used to get up early with Anita and get ready to go to work. Sometimes he felt comfortable in his office. However, something used to bother him a lot. His office was across from the office of the chief editor, the one who was in charge of the accommodation for the employers. Quite often he passed the hall and found himself in front of that door. He was led by his pride to act like horses do.

He had a limited view around him, even though the rubber blinders on the sides of his eyes were missing. He wasn't aware of many of the other things going on around him such as the lives of the people around him, the gossip inside the coffee shop, the intrigues, the anonymous letters and lists hidden in the bureaucrat drawers. A horse could be treated in any way the boss wanted to treat him.

He could even change his character, if the boss wanted him to do so. Even as nothing changed in his appearance or in his bones, destined to be burdened. With the patience of a horse, he tried to bear the weight of the daily carriage. Unable to manage the weight, Daniel developed a hunch on his back. However, he was smart as a horse, (if it is proven that horses are smart). He couldn't imagine that the world was so full of infamy and that the truth can be twisted. As he was chewing his fodder in the evening, he thought of rebuilding his old, stinky stall. This was the way the state awarded its devoted servant, he thought. This is the prize for being faithful and honest. Regardless, someone has to work for the government, he thought; maybe this someone has to be flexible. Maybe a chameleon could do a better job. Otherwise, he has to die as a sick horse dwelling in that old, ruined hospital.

So far Daniel had gained a lot of experience. He was still patient. But one day rheumatism and asthma got the better of him. The doctors grabbed him by his legs and arms and took him into the hospital. On the other side, they didn't think that he could get any better. His bones were pierced by hundreds of hot imaginary pins and needles. The hallucinations gave him nausea. He didn't even want to look at the lunch, especially the meat made him sick, although the people tried to convince him that the meat they cooked for him was carved from a cow or a lamb. The food used to get stuck in his throat as the idea of dying stayed in his mind.

This hospital for humans differed from the animal's hospital. The halls and the rooms were cleaned and the shelters always set up. The doctors and the nurses always wore white suits. Sometimes he thought they would throw him out and dump him in a trash bag. He had the weirdest desire one could have.

He wanted to be dumped in a sausage factory, where flesh of his body would be waiting to be ground up. He imagined people eating and chewing with thousands of teeth the sausages made out of his flesh. The sausages then would move down to their stomachs and pellets would travel into the toilets, pipes and end down in the sea. He had no problems at all setting up this entire story. Sometimes he was transformed into water, grass and later on, into a horse again. He never did feel tired of going through this process many times. Daniel was so involved in this game, such that many months went by.

One day the boss told him that he had been fired. It was a big shock to him. He felt powerless, unimportant and unable to take action. The evenings when he had sex with Anita had come to an end. Anita seemed to be far away from him. Moreover, he didn't want to have sex. He had no desire. The environment he lived in was spoiled by different kinds of medications, thus paralyzing his sexual and emotional feelings. Now life seemed to be a boring movie, where no words could be understood.

He was aware that the hospital for horses was an inseparable part of his body; it was like an unbelievable ghost under the burning sun of the desert. He was always skeptical and waiting to hide in his cave. Surprisingly enough, the day of his release from the hospital approached soon. He went again to his own shelter at the hospital. Instead of having fun, bad luck followed him everywhere. Daniel was still sick and now unemployed. He had a terrible thought in his mind. He imagined his wife becoming pregnant and giving birth to a little pony. That's why he was always very careful and afraid to have sex with her anymore.

As he was lying on his bed on a Saturday evening, Anita came close to him and put her arms around his neck. Daniel stayed very quiet and cold. He pushed his wife away a little and turned his back. Anita was embarrassed to see her husband behaving that way. She grabbed him by his shoulder, but Daniel still stayed on his side like a rock, without showing any feeling. Then she decided to slap him on the back of his head with her little soft hand. He turned to her and stared at her totally surprised.

"What's up?" he asked her.

"What's up with you? Why don't you talk to me? Would you please explain to me what's going on around here?"

"Nothing! What's the matter with you? You got crazy?"

"You call me 'crazy?'"

"No, I am not calling you 'crazy.' I am tired."

"Tired of doing what?"

"I am tired of myself. I am tired of these walls!"

"And you are tired of me? Are you tired of me?"

"No, I am not tired of you. You are the only thing I got. Come on honey, give me a break."

"You don't like me anymore!" Anita replied and covered her face with both hands and cried. Her body shivered as Daniel sat on his bed. He didn't know what to say and for the moment thought it would be better not to talk, but just to keep quiet. He was not feeling in a good mood to argue with her.

"If I tell her that I am horse now, she is going to freak out. She is going to leave me for good. Maybe it's a good idea, what she just said that I don't like her. He turned his back, but Anita stopped sobbing and screamed at him.

"Tell me, what's happening to you? Why do you stay so quiet and passive? Since you came out from the hospital, you are not the same person I met," Anita replied. Her eyes were full with tears and her hair was messed up. She still looked like a beautiful woman with those blue eyes and curly black hair.

"Do you want to know the whole truth?"

"Yes, I want to know the whole truth!"

"This hospital is for horses, it's not a house where we can live together as a husband and wife. These barracks are eating me alive. I think I am a horse now, not the Daniel that you used to know!"

"You are what?"

"You heard me! I am a horse now! Not a human, but an animal. A dirty animal! Do you want to sleep with a big horse in your bed? These walls changed me. This air changed me. I keep seeing dreams with the horse running back and forth on the streets, coming out from this building. I see wounded horses, dead horses, their corpses all over the place. I am afraid that if we had sex, you might become pregnant with me and a little pony is gonna come out from your belly within nine months," Daniel yelled and stared at her like he had never done before.

"Are you saying that you are having hallucinations?" Anita asked him as her jaw dropped a little.

"These are not hallucinations! This is the new reality that I have lived for several months now. I am warning you. If we don't leave from here, I am going to be a real animal. Our marriage will be a disaster."

"Our marriage is a disaster already, you should know that. You lost your job. You are staying away from me and now you want to leave us without a roof over our heads. What else is next, tell me? You don't love me anymore."

"I love you, honey!"

"You love me, but you don't want to stay with me under this roof, right?"

"Anita, we have to leave from here. Then you will start recognizing me again as the guy you always knew."

"Where do you want us to go, in the street? Do you have a clue how much an apartment for rent would cost us? My salary is three hundred dollars per month and the rent is almost three hundred dollars. One person has to work just for the rent, forget the rest."

"First we can go to my parents' house. We live there for some time, until I feel better. Then I'll find another job and we can start from the beginning," Daniel said and grabbed Anita by both hands and held them tight.

"There is no job around here. Look around, many companies have shut their doors. Everybody is leaving. They are taking boats to go to Italy. Some other people like us cross the border through the mountains, walking for several days to go to Greece. Some other people sell their homes to buy a visa to go to Canada. You have to open your eyes and see. Where do you live, my love?"

"I don't exactly know where I live. I know something for sure. If we don't abandon this place, our whole future will be in danger. Let's take the first step. We simply leave from here. Let's go to my parents'. We can do the same thing that other people did; we can go overseas too."

"We can go overseas, but not in your parents' home."

"We have to leave now. Where are we going to leave now?" Daniel screamed.

"Sheaths! Why do you scream? We can go to my parents' home. They have a bigger space. Our room is still untouched," Anita said.

"I don't mind to come to your parents', but not more than two weeks. Are you happy now?"

"What about the money? I am not going to ask my parents for money," she panicked.

"We are going to walk across the border and go to Greece and find a job. I know it is going to be hard for both of us, but at the end everything will be just fine," Daniel said with a new light in his eyes. His hands were shivering, as he was standing in the middle of the room. Anita came closer to him, as Daniel kissed her lips. She sighed.

"I am still afraid, that you are still going to have those weird hallucinations," she said.

Daniel dropped his arms from her wrist and walked around the room, counting the steps.

"Are you still afraid that I am going to have the same hallucinations? Really?"

"Yes, at the end all our sacrifices will go in vain. You will not change. You better see a doctor again."

"I might not change if we stay here. Before we go we have to set this hospital on fire," he added all of a sudden.

"On fire?"

"Yes! Now! I spray it with gas all over the place and get a small lighter and put it on fire. I want to see the fire with my eyes before we leave."

"Are you gone mad?"

"Yes I am mad! I don't want to live like this anymore. Please Anita, say "yes" and I'll be all yours. That's the only magic, which would save me from myself," Daniel said.

Anita held her head with her fists. That was the only roof they had and Daniel wanted to blow it from the foundations. Was it just too much?

"What do you say?" Daniel insisted.

"We can keep the place. We can repair it, when we come back from Greece. We can privatize it after we collect some money and we can build a new home at the same place. Don't you think it's smarter this way?" Anita said.

"I don't want to see this place anymore. Even if we build a new house on the same spot, I'll still hear the horses coming to their hospital. This place belongs to them; that's why they are punishing us."

"Who is punishing us?"

"The souls of the dead horses!"

"Then let's put it on fire and we go!" Anita decided instinctively.

"Let's start packing!" Daniel said and jumped off the bed.

There was not too much stuff in their room. It took them only a couple of hours to get everything ready. Daniel grabbed a container filled with liquid gas and sprayed the place from top to bottom. He lit a cigarette and threw it right in the middle of the room. Huge tongues of fire licked the hospital of the horses.

Without turning his head to look behind him, Daniel Shkurti hugged his wife Anita and they ran as fast as they could from there.

THE FIRST LINE OF DUTY

The army trucks moved slowly away from *CFB Trenton Airfield* towards highway 401, carrying the caskets of soldiers who had fallen in Afghanistan. Hundreds of people crowded both sides of the road. Vanessa Melo tried not to cry as she drove her Honda Civic, looking at all the people standing along the shoulder. There was no way she could miss such an important moment in her life, honouring the body of Roberto Silva, her childhood friend. Robert had asked her to marry him three weeks ago.

Roberto was from Azores Island and had come to Canada when he was five-years-old. He met Vanessa two years ago at a wedding ceremony in a Portuguese church. They attended the same high school and lived in the same neighbourhood. They would often see each other, sometimes saying, "hi" and "bye," as they passed. Over time, their friendship became stronger, and eventually evolved into a romance.

Vanessa remembered the day when Roberto left Canada for Afghanistan. She gave him a ride to the military base, telling him that she didn't want him to go, and that many people were getting killed. Roberto listened to her carefully and promised her that he was going to come back soon.

"It won't last too long," he said. "I'll write you a letter as soon as I get there. Actually, I am going to write you whenever I have a chance."

Vanessa had a bad feeling that she was not going to see him again. "You promise?" she said, lips quavering.

"I promise." Roberto squeezed her in his arms, pulling away, only to wipe her tears.

Roberto kept his promise. He sent her letters every week for six months.

Vanessa was always that delicate and skinny girl, who had no idea that part of the world even existed. But with his letters, Afghanistan became so vivid and real. Names like, *Kabul, Kandahar, Tora Bora, Bin Laden, Taliban,* and *Hamid Karzai,* were added to her daily vocabulary. She imagined his smiling image through the lines in the letters sent to her from the front line of fire.

She remembered his last letter, dated May 15th, 2010. "Dear Vanessa, I had a close call today. Our truck was fully loaded with soldiers, when a land-mine exploded in the middle of the road. Three soldiers from my platoon were wounded. Thank God their wounds are not life threatening. I swear, your image appeared in front of me at that moment. Your eyes were shining and you had a white dress on. You didn't speak, just smiled to me and disappeared into the woods. Then I woke up and saw myself on the side of the road, right on top of the wounded soldiers. I escaped with just a scratch on my left cheek, and that was it."

Then one Monday morning, Vanessa went out to check the mail and found it empty. She stood in front of the mailbox, shaking, certain that something had happened to Roberto. Pushing the thought out of her head, she returned to check the mailbox each morning, and still, nothing. On the second Monday, there were still no letters from Roberto. She couldn't think of any excuses why he wouldn't write and felt anxious.

Vanessa kept watching the news on CP24, praying to God that nothing had happened to him. Three other soldiers had lost their lives in Afghanistan a week before, and their bodies were expected to come home soon.

His mother had been informed officially by the military command of the peacekeeping force in Afghanistan, and had called Vanessa immediately. She felt the spit drying in her mouth as her hand holding the receiver shook involuntarily.

"His body will be arriving tomorrow," said his mother.

"No, this can't be happening," said Vanessa in disbelief. "How?"

"We don't know. They will bring his body to the church tomorrow at four o'clock."

Vanessa woke the next morning, believing it all to be a bad dream. The family was waiting at the Portuguese Catholic Church on Dundas for Roberto's body to return home, but Vanessa wanted to be the first to pay tribute to him. She decided to go to the Highway of Heroes, where every Monday the cortège of the fallen soldiers arrived. She was half way to CFB Trenton Airfield when she felt the urge to change the station. Over the speaker she heard the newscaster announcing that Roberto Silva had lost his life, attacking a terrorist base, just outside Kandahar.

"Oh God," she cried, pulling over, turning off the ignition. "He was such a wonderful soul!" Sobbing, she hit the steering wheel. "He wasn't the type of guy to go to war and fight. He was just an ordinary young man who got caught in the wrong place, at the wrong time. He was a skilled bricklayer. He could build a million dollar house. It was his passion and pride."

Vanessa remembered their last night out together, drinking a couple of beers at the Euro Sports Bar on Dundas.

"As soon as I am back, we are going to Niagara Falls," he said, taking a sip of his *Sagres*. "I wish I could watch the waterfall with you, once again."

Her hands were shivering and her forehead was covered with sweat. She took a deep breath and grabbed the red flowers that she had bought from the back seat. Looking around, she realized that the crowd was mostly older people, who were barely standing on their feet, kids, and young women in tears.

"Our dead soldiers are coming home. Our dead soldiers! May God Bless their souls!" an old man said, standing next to her.

Vanessa bent over the bridge to have a better view of the trucks, loaded with the coffins of the dead soldiers, hoping she could see Roberto's casket.

Ordinary people came out of their homes and lined both sides of the road, holding Canadian flags and flowers. Vanessa tried to read the names written on the caskets, but it was impossible. The bridge was too high above the highway and she could not tell which coffin belonged to Roberto.

"These guys gave their last breath, without even knowing why they were there," she heard someone saying. She turned her head to see who was talking. It was an old man standing next to her.

"Hi, my name is Jerry," he introduced himself with tears in his eyes. "I got a notice from the army that my grandson is coming home today. He was killed a week ago in Kabul. They were checking an abandoned home when a land-mine exploded in the backyard. They collected him piece by piece, just so they could put him in a casket. He was my daughter's only son."

Vanessa turned and hugged him.

"I have a question for you," Jerry said. "Is our mission in Afghanistan worth it?"

Vanessa didn't feel she could answer him. She was feeling tired, almost exhausted. She threw the flowers from the bridge down to the cortège. The flowers missed the trucks. She turned to Jerry, said *goodbye*, and got in her car. Her hands shivered on the wheel as she tried to concentrate on driving.

It was time. She made the drive to the church. Many people were gathered out front. Roberto's casket had just arrived. His relatives and friends were all there, paying tribute to him. A group of military men from the Canadian Armed Forces was carrying the casket.

Vanessa parked the car and rushed to get into the crowd. She saw Roberto's mother, Fortina, being helped by two women. They were holding her by the arms, as the soldiers tried to get through. Vanessa stopped in front of the casket and kissed it. She touched it with her fingers and turned to Fortina. She hugged the old woman and looked toward the sky for an answer. Nothing was there, not even a cloud.

She stood in front of the casket after they had lifted the lid. Roberto was a big guy, heavy and serious even in death. He was lying peacefully surrounded by flowers. His face was clean and serene. She kissed his forehead, which was cold like a gravestone. "*Adieus*'," she thought she heard him say.

"*Adieus*, Roberto," she repeated back to him and went into the crowd looking for Fortina.

***P.I. (Përparim) Kapllani** is from Albania, where he was a well-known journalist, worked as an anti-aircraft gun officer and teacher of Literature and Albanian. Kapllani is the author of three books in English,* The Last Will—a novel*;* Beyond the Edge—short stories*, and* Queen Teuta of Illyria—a play. *He published four books in the Albanian language and has been included in two anthologies. His fifth book in Albanian entitled* Mbretneshë Teuta e Ilirisë *will be published in print and ebook by In Our Words Inc. in October 2014.*

Zohra Zoberi

CHOREOGRAPHING A BREAKTHROUGH!

Having lost *everything*, coping
with yet another night of insomnia
sluggishly I descend
heavily down the wooden stairway
step   by step   by step
        Financially *'fondled'*
        Emotionally *'embezzled'*
        Physically *'frazzled'*
        A potent mixture—feeling as though I could explode,
        breakdown, or maybe ... disintegrate?
Lethargic, I plunked myself
upon the living room sofa   barely conscious.
                        Suddenly I felt a presence
                        mysterious, majestic, mystical
                        arms outstretched as though
                        reaching out to rescue me
        The Tall Evergreen
        beside my living room window
        a symphony of epiphany!
                Thunder, lightning, the ice storm of last winter
                he too has weathered
                the harshest of all weathers
        I hear him whisper:
        "Why not choreograph YOUR own breakthrough?"
        I toss and turn at first
        my soul yearns
        I reach for my stereo
                exchange a glance with him
                Sun shines   through it light of hope is shimmering
                though sigh of relief is languid but ...
        Cool breeze makes the branches dance   it cheers me
        I re-adjust soft cushions   fall asleep.

Yet another wakeful night
footsteps sound the gravity of fatigue
I descend step by step by step
and there he stands, Adamant beauty enhanced
in the backdrop of pale rose horizon the waking sky
prompts me to contemplation meditation
day after day after day
coaxing, cajoling my muse till I give in
Language of the Universe I begin to interpret
Reflection on my grey wall is green,
around its edges are rainbow colours, why?
Holding hands each day now habitual
Week after week he makes me
travel into past and present
to Bueau mountain in Cameroun
where from Cloud *Ten*, I looked upon *Nine*
Vienna Philharmonic Orchestra plays
in my fond memories
Vivid imagination of a bright future I foresee
How this evergreen inspires:
on a day of sad tidings of dark clouds even when this
evergreen turns blue
it stands firm, rooted to the ground
knowing that the rain will come and go, as tears
will nurture the roots
leaves will shine so will my spirit
How he alters my perception each day:
In reality I haven't lost anything
all that's in nature forever belongs to me
Spontaneously I dance my way out barefoot on moist green
singing birds are flocking, like my aspirations
I am that blue spruce
from a family of Evergreens

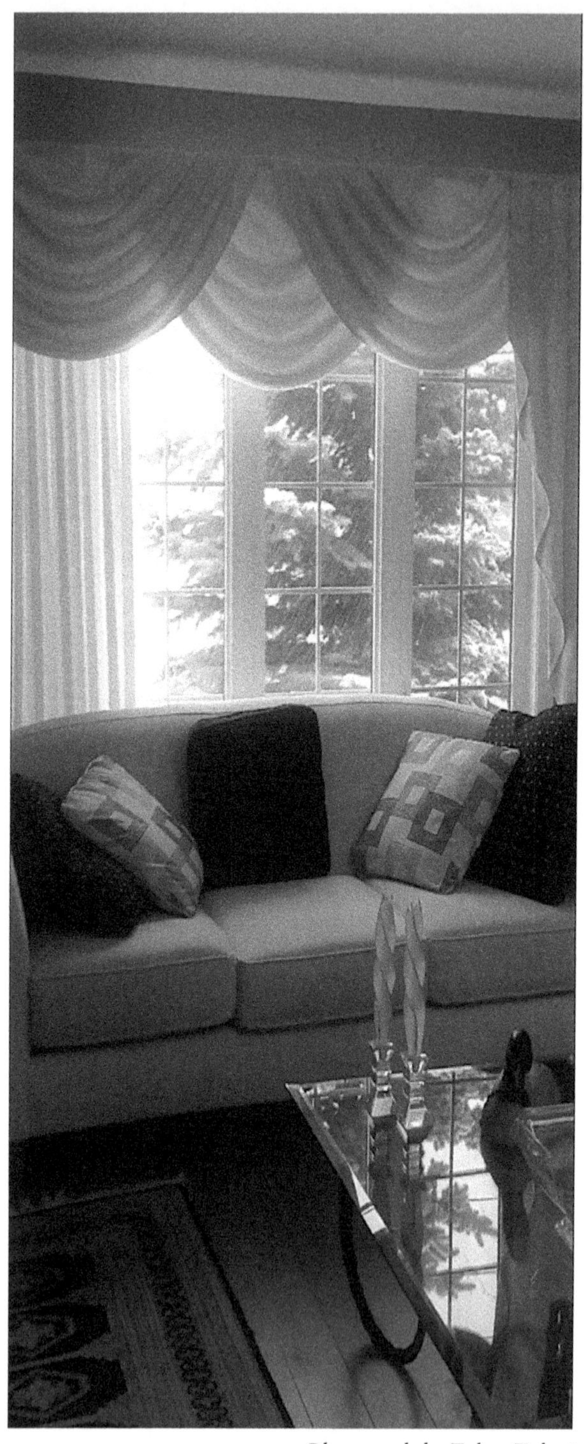

Photograph by Zohra Zoberi

CATCH TWENTY-TWO

Her sleeveless, bare-midriff blouses and 'hipster' *saris* offered a stunning sight that was a source of delight to many watchful eyes. Dimpled cheeks, olive complexion, captivating brown eyes and long satiny hair all conspired to knock ten years off of Saajda's actual forty.

Saajda wasn't just vanity personified; there was also an enviable intellectual side to her. She was adept at reciting poetry appropriate to the occasion; telling jokes in the most appealing way, and she could discuss world politics with singular confidence. Adding to our delight was the fact that she was also an accomplished sitar player who was generally willing to entertain any of our requests.

It is often said, rather tongue-in-cheek, about men: '*who isn't fond of his own child and another man's wife?*' As for Saajda, it was not just our husbands who were beguiled by her; we women were totally captivated too.

Even those women who could have otherwise been insecure and jealous of her were not, because Saajda had a spiritual side to her that appealed to everyone. She would take the time to discover our personal issues and concerns and if any of us needed anything, we could count on Saajda to quickly bring us the right information.

She was always manicured and pedicured to perfection before she adorned herself in exquisite jewellery and designer shoes. The only thing that seemed not to fit the image was 'the old purse' hanging beside her known as Zulfiqar, her husband; an unassuming, slender, harmless-looking man who attracted neither anyone's attention nor animosity. If anyone envied him, it was for his 'spirited,' best dressed and most fashionable prize possession that was always the life of the party, be it an all-night-long private musical evening, a dance party or just a friendly dinner.

In the hope of receiving similar favours for themselves, wives of controlling husbands often tried to point out her good fortune to their spouses. "How lucky she is that Zulfi has no objection to what she does and where she goes. She is free to enjoy life's greatest pleasures."

At the end of the dinner parties, we would invariably spot one or two people eagerly approaching Saajda:

"Let us know whenever you're available. We would love to invite you over for our next get-together. Could you give me your number?"

She had a hard time refusing all the invitations but there are only so many weekends in a year.

Then, all of a sudden, Saajda disappeared from her entire circle of friends, leaving us baffled as to what became of her. Why wouldn't her husband contact us? Was she kidnapped? What happened to their little eight-year-old daughter, Sana? Did they just up and leave town?

One day, out of the blue, our friend Zarina called: "You'll never believe the news." Then she went silent.

"For sure I won't believe it if I don't hear it. Tell me, tell me!"

"Alright but it's hard to believe… Saajda and Zulfiqar are getting a divorce."

"Divorce?" I was in shock. She was right. It was hard to believe.

"And wait, there's more still. Saajda not only initiated the divorce but she's suing her husband for raping her."

"What? How can a woman sue her own husband for rape?"

I was too naive to understand that this could even be a possibility.

"Well, if he forces her into action and she's not willing, don't you think it constitutes rape?" replied Zarina. She was obviously much more knowledgeable than I.

"I guess so." It still took a while for the thought to register. We were always taught that a woman must fulfill her husband's physical needs at all times; and if she refuses him when he's in the mood, the angels will curse her all night long.

I kept my true reaction to myself and commented: "Everyone believed that Zulfiqar brought the world under his wife's feet. He was such a gentleman, a harmless soul."

"Really? Well, would you believe that he was caught molesting young girls in their apartment building? Apparently Saajda had known this for some time but it's only now that she found the courage to take some action."

"I still find it hard to believe. You're saying that Zulfiqar turned out to be a... pedophile?"

Zarina wasted no time in imparting the news to the rest of our friends and soon it became the topic of everyday conversation. It bothered me that they seemed to be enjoying that gossip a little too much.

A few weeks later that we found out that Saajda's divorce had been quickly finalized.

Since her family was thousands of miles away, she had moved in with one of her friends Cynthia...a name we had never even heard before? Saajda enrolled in Sheridan College to train as a medical secretary and was also looking for a job.

Our circle of friends remained intact and after several months, we almost forgot Saajda ever existed. Samina had gladly taken over her role as the centre of everyone's attention. Despite much effort to copy her dressing style and even repeating some of her poetic phrases, Samina was no replacement for our enchanting loss.

One day Samina brought surprising but rather pleasant news to us: "Believe it or not, Saajda met an amazing gentleman on a flight from Toronto to Denmark and she fell in love. His name is Imtiaz, he's two years younger than her… and they're getting married."

"What? Getting married, to a younger guy? Lucky devil!"

When marriages are arranged by our elders, a difference of at least five years is traditionally considered ideal. 'Women age faster,' they say. In any case, I also thought that Saajda was one lucky lady who not only got rid of her 'old purse,' but also found the love of her life in a short span of time. *A younger man, wow!*

I couldn't hold back my delight and curiosity. In fact, I was determined to meet with her and find out for myself.

"You have no idea what I've been through all these months," she confided to me during our first encounter.

"But we thought you were the happiest of us all. How come you never shared your pain with us?"

"Share what, that my harmless looking, meek little husband was a child molester? That I was scared to leave my daughter alone with her father? These were facts I couldn't even face myself."

"But I'm glad you eventually did something about it, Saajda. Some families simply freak out at the thought of divorce, but thank God your family cooperated."

"You've no idea what a struggle it was to convince them… but they finally accepted the truth. If it wasn't for my father, I'd still be stuck with Zulfiqar. My mom kept telling me, "Maybe it's just your imagination. He has a man's blood in his veins and you'll see in a few years he will calm down. Try to overlook it."

"Can you believe that?" Saajda was overcome with emotion.

"How can a mother say that to her own daughter?"

"Because her biggest concern is 'what would *others* say?'"

"Well, I'm glad at least your father was on your side."

"The day I confided in my father, he ordered Zulfiqar out of my sight. Within two weeks, my father flew from Lahore to Toronto, rented a place downtown for a month, and arranged temporary accommodation for me and Sana until my friend Cynthia invited us to move in with her."

"Cynthia? Your best friend that we never heard about?" My voice dripped sarcasm. After an uncomfortable silence, I continued:

"Well, at least tell me about this handsome hunk you accidentally met and fell for on a flight. Is it true you're already engaged? And if so, when is the wedding?"

"Here," Saajda leaned forward to show off her engagement ring with pride. "It's the first time a man has made me feel like a real woman. He put me on a pedestal and in Copenhagen his whole family flocked around us, raving over me. You've no idea how happy I felt. Imtiaz is extremely caring, and so romantic too, and he...he really knows how to respect a woman." Saajda was delighted to talk about all his special qualities.

"But... we all thought Zulfiqar was the same."

"Camouflage, my dear. It was just camouflage. Beneath that innocent image resided a devil."

"I'm happy for you that your agony is over… but... but...I really hope that Imtiaz is all that you tell me he is. In any case, when and where is the wedding and I hope we're going to be invited."

Imtiaz's parents lived in Denmark so in the ensuing weeks, Saajda and Imtiaz's cousins and uncles from India and Pakistan, flew all the way to Denmark to attend the grand wedding. Saajda's parents went to great lengths to make her wedding day even more special than the first time. They prepared a fancy *jahaiz* (dowry) all over again. Guilt-ridden, they expressed their regret about her first marriage by saying, "We messed up her life by arranging her marriage without investigating Zulfiqar's family background, and our poor daughter had to suffer in silence."

In the following months, we received details of Saajda's grand wedding in Denmark from various sources. I even saw a photograph of the couple with her charming daughter sitting between the bride and groom, looking quite happy. Her dream man had accepted the fact that Saajda and her nine-year-old girl came as a package.

The immigration application process was facilitated due to the marriage and Imtiaz was able to move to Canada. Saajda's friends held a small reception for the bride and groom in Toronto. It was evident that several of our friends at the reception envied her. "Can you see the glow of new love on her face?" one whispered longingly.

"I think I too should consider this option," another said; and I had to wonder if she was really joking or not.

We wasted no time in putting our heads together at the party to plan and extend a dinner invitation to the new couple, at Zarina's place.

Knowing how Saajda was always decked out for any occasion, we all made a point to dress up in our fanciest style to honour the newly-weds. Each of us made our specialty dish and we went out of our way to order a beautiful cake with the names of the happy couple engraved in icing. To suit her exquisite taste, we lit candles and had sitar music playing in the background as we anxiously awaited their arrival.

Finally the doorbell rang and there she was. Much to our surprise, all dressed in plain, dull brown, Western attire, as opposed to her usual multi-coloured, gossamer *saris.* The hosts were overdressed and the guest of honour was exceptionally underdressed for the woman we all knew. Throughout the night, she remained strangely silent which made it an intriguing and oddly disturbing evening for us all.

After that event, she never phoned in her usual thank-you, nor did she return anyone's calls.

I phoned her work number and got the reply, "Sorry she doesn't work here any longer."

I then called her landlord, who also replied, "Sorry, they don't live here anymore."

Saajda had become a mystery to us all once again.

A few weeks later, while I was shopping at the Bay, I spotted a young woman wearing *Hijaab* and *Abaya*. I was taken aback when for an instant; I thought I recognized the face. I shook my head and smiled as I realized it couldn't possibly have been Saajda. It was just someone that resembled her. Then as I watched the dowdy-covered woman walk away, I remembered how sensual and exotic Saajda always looked in those sleeveless tops and hipster saris. I thought about her cheerful and beguiling presence and I was relieved to conclude that this woman couldn't possibly be the same person.

Then one day, I ran into the same woman … but this time at my doctor's office.

She ignored me once again, but this time, I was certain, there was no mistake; so I dared to confront her:

"How can you ignore me as if I never existed? You and I were such good friends. How could you disappear without a word? Didn't you think I would notice or care?"

Saajda's eyes welled up with tears and she stammered as she tried to speak.

"I-I can't talk right now… so… so maybe later." She hurried away but not before handing me her phone number and some words of caution. "Don't call me in the evenings." That got me a bit apprehensive about her newfound love.

Two weeks after that, we finally got together over a coffee at Tim Hortons. I asked her directly:

"Are you having marital problems again?"

"Imtiaz is a wonderful man."

"But...?"

"He is still working things out."

That made me highly suspicious.

"Is he mean to you? Has he turned out to be an alcoholic or something?"

"Neither of the above" She lowered her gaze.

"Does he abuse you?"

"On the contrary."

"What's the matter then? I just know something is very wrong, so please, just blurt it out." She remained silent… so I carried on.

"Look at you, you're a changed person. I feel like I'm sitting in front of someone I've never met."

"I know it's the Hijaab. It's my *appearance* isn't it? But I've changed in many other ways too."

I thought it best not to pursue this subject at this time, so I reverted to discussing other issues.

"So Saajda, tell me please, what went wrong with your...um...Mr. Ideal."

"In many ways he *is* Mr. Ideal. I told you he's a fine gentleman who can truly respect a woman. He's proper and polite and has no qualms about helping around the house. He loves to cook."

"Then what is it?" I was beginning to get impatient.

"It's just that, Imtiaz isn't...he's not...um."

"He isn't what? Tell me, please."

"He's not ...um... not interested in women."

"He's what?" I choked. "I don't believe it. Then why did he marry you?"

"Family pressure. He had to get them off his back! In Denmark, he was surrounded by his traditional family, so it was difficult to...eh… But now…"

"… But now what?" I was shocked but intensely curious.

"Over here in Canada he feels free. Mainly because his family isn't around so... he's finally..."

"Finally what?" I had to hear HER say it out loud, so I could believe it.

"... Out of the closet," Saajda finally purged herself of the secret that he is gay. "He has a lot of friends here on Church Street."

Only women from my culture would understand that in this day and age a divorced woman would agree to marry someone without being physically intimate first. I kept that thought to myself.

We remained silent for an uncomfortable few seconds. I finally succumbed to asking the question that was pounding in my head.

"So, are you getting divorced again?"

"We are … already divorced." She went on: "Although he tried to convince me to stay together. Said he may not be able to give me everything I would want in a man but he can promise to remain a good and loyal friend and more important..."

"… More important? What could be more important?"

"… the fact that around him my daughter would be safe. After what I went through in my last marriage, her safety is of the utmost importance to me."

"Saajda, are you telling me that you didn't feel cheated by this man?"

"Of course I did but … what could he do? We're both caught in this catch twenty-two. So we considered a compromise."

"How was it a compromise?"

"Divorced twice is a double stigma, don't you know it. My mom would have a heart attack."

"So he thought you could help each other out, a friend in need is that it? Okay, I'm glad you didn't fall for that 'compromise' marital arrangement. Now look me in the eye and tell me what about this new fashion statement of yours?"

"I had to somehow find an outlet for my frustration and..."

"...and for that you have to change your identity? This Abaya isn't exactly a Pakistani or Indian outfit my dear… and for your outlet what about your passion for sitar, do you still play it?"

"No, no more. Music is...um..."

"...*Haraam*?" I completed it for her with a taste of bitterness dripping from my tongue. "I knew it, I just knew it. Did it ever occur to you that casting aside God-given talent might be an even bigger sin? How could you veer so far away from who you are, Saajda? Who got to you?"

"It's Sister Rabia who gives *Durse* (*religious sermons at women's gatherings*). After Imtiaz left, one day she found me crying my heart out and she was kind enough to extend a 'sympathetic ear.' More like counselling. So here I am now …a changed person who has finally found peace."

Peace!

While I was making every effort to digest Saajda's words, a memory came to me of Farzana, a sweet lady I once knew, who had to endure her husband's announcement that he was leaving her for another woman, in the same week she was grieving the loss of her mother. Farzana too had been 'rescued' by the religious well-wishers in the community. Now it was clear that Saajda had been extended a similar 'sympathetic ear' in a vulnerable time in her life.

She sadly and quietly repeated: "But he was a fine gentleman who can truly respect a woman."

Zohra Zoberi *is the Artistic Director of Bridging the Gap (Enlightenment through Entertainment). Zohra writes poetry, prose and plays in two languages (Urdu and English). Recognized by the Government of Ontario for raising awareness through her award winning socio dramas staged in Canada. An 'All Rounder' who won gold medals in sports, Top National Sales Award in Banking (CIBC), as well as Literary Arts and Performing Arts awards from the Mississauga Arts Council. Published in numerous anthologies, her second book* True Colours—From the Universe to the Inner Mind *is an eclectic collection of prose poems. Zohra is the recipient of Ambassador of Peace award (Universal Peace Federation) and 'Woman's Courage' award (Endless Possibilities 2012).*

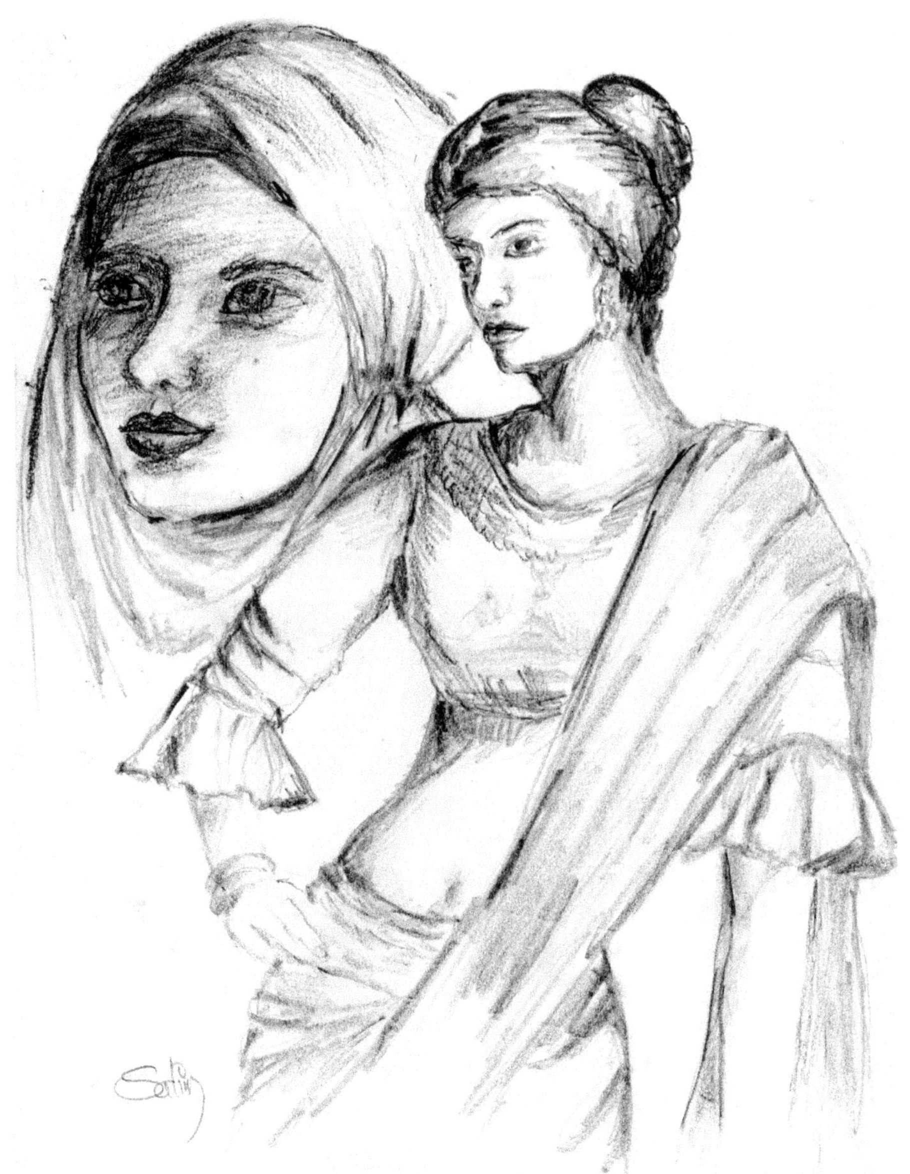

Illustration by Salim Khan

Trevor Trower

TALE OF THE DEAD CAT

A lot of people dote on their pets, and that's all right; sometimes they get more love and affection from their cat or dog than they ever get from a fellow human.

The airline company I used to work for makes a lot of money carrying pets from one place to another. Special arrangements are made to satisfy the customer's needs when caring for the traveling pet. There are ways to get special dispensation and allow certain animals to travel in the passenger cabin, but that does not happen often. A working dog has the legal right to travel with its owner in the cabin when flying and, in that situation, does not need to be caged.

A special area in the aircraft cargo hold is reserved for the animal passenger and is air-conditioned and pressurized. The animal must be caged and it is often, for obvious reasons, tranquillized so it will not be stressed by the strange environment. The flight attendant is alerted that an animal is on board, and can reassure the owner that his or her pet is comfortable. The ramp personnel go out of their way to give the travelling pet all the appropriate TLC. When there is an interruption in the flight, there is always a kindly soul to provide the pet with fresh water and, in some cases, even exercise. Yes, my company goes to extreme lengths to satisfy the customer.

During my career of 35 years with the airline, I have had a lot of experiences with travelling animals; I've cared for dogs and cats on many occasions, but also monkeys, swans, snakes, macaws, and even horses and prize cattle and, on one occasion, half a million day-old chicks on a 747 to Egypt.

Sadly, all handling of this special cargo is not successful. I have often wondered if a pet were to die enroute would the customer get the fare refunded. In the event a human passenger dies in flight, I know for a fact that they don't get their money back. We certainly never guarantee 'arrive alive' as a slogan, but come to think of it, what a great slogan that would be.

As often happens when chatting with fellow retired employees at our monthly coffee klatch, stories are told that make you laugh, cry or just wonder. And my friend Bob, who always has a tale to tell, once again brought on a fit of laughter when he told the tale of the dead cat.

When flight 148 arrived from Vancouver that day, Jan the big Dutch agent, went out to the plane to bring the cat into the baggage area in preparation for its delivery to the customer. The cat box was carefully transported to our office, and because there was no movement in the box, we carefully opened it. Sure enough, we found that the cat was dead, stiff as a board. Jan had been involved with a dead animal on a previous occasion and had no intention of going through that kind of investigation again. He sensibly thought, there can't be a lot of differences between cats, and as there were several cats hanging about the premises keeping down the mice, he would catch one that looked the same as the dead one and replace it, and everybody would be happy.

A phone call was made to the person living in Toronto to whom the cat was addressed, telling the lady that her cat had arrived from VR, and she could collect it any time. In the meantime, Jan and several of the staff went on the hunt around the building, looking for the replacement for the dead tabby. Well, sure enough, a friendly cat who looked like the dead cat was found and put in the travelling cat box and placed on the counter, waiting to be picked up. Everyone went about their work, satisfied that they had solved a serious problem for the company. Jan even got a pat on the back for his resourcefulness.

Well, it was not much later that the lady arrived for the cat and when it was handed to her and she saw the live cat, she screamed in horror and shouted, "That's not my cat, my cat is dead; it was sent here so I could have it stuffed."

Only with the best of good fortune, Jan was able to retrieve the dead cat from the trash and carefully carry it to its rightful owner, who accepted the explanations with good humour.

***Trevor Trower** was born in Southampton, England in 1927. Educated in Plymouth and Toronto and retired after 35 years with Air Canada In-Flight Service. His hobbies include short story and poetry writing.*

His published books include The Traveling Man, The Early Days, *2006;* The Traveling Man, an Air Canada memoir, *2008;* Poetry For Everyday Use, *2009;* A Sea Of Pink Blossoms, *2011. A number of short stories and poems have been published in magazines and on the web at BBC North Wales. Married for 57 years to dear wife Kathleen, with five children and ten grandchildren. He currently lives in Georgetown, Ontario.*

Cheryl Antao-Xavier

SOPHIA

It was not until I saw my neighbour across the street standing at the edge of her driveway, craning to look at something outside my house that I suddenly became aware of the sound of a baby wailing. I dashed downstairs and yanked open the front door. The wailing was a high-pitched scream by then, resounding off the porch walls. A tiny babe lay in an old battered car seat, covered by a faded pink baby blanket, a shock of black hair, a face bluish purple from the screaming and tiny fists clenched white.

My heart cringed. Oh my God, I know whose baby this is.

I picked up the car seat and wrestled it through the storm door. The baby was whimpering by now. Running out of steam, I guessed. Poor, poor kid.

"Shall I call the police?" My pesky neighbour was at the door. "Whose baby is it? Do you know whose baby it is?"

"It's mine now," I said and shut the door in her face.

"Shall I call the police?" she yelled through the door.

By the time the police arrived, I had mixed some formula from the trial packs I found tucked in the car seat. The baby was drinking hungrily, but every few minutes she jerked as if startled, stopped drinking, wailed and then began drinking again as I held her close and rocked her.

Five hours later my husband and two sons were home, and the police were still there, asking questions. Did I know the mother? Did I have any idea whose baby it was? The pesky neighbour gave them more information than I did. She knew all the goings-on on Bremen Lane. But even she had missed the arrival of the baby on our doorstep.

"Did the mother leave a name for the baby?" asked the Child Services woman, who was going through the contents of the car seat.

"Her name is Sophia," I said.

"What? What?" my husband and the reporting police officer said in unison, "How do you know that?"

"We will give her that name when she comes to live with us."

Six months of wrangling with Children's Services, with courts and interminable red tape, but finally Sophia was mine. Ours. By the time she came through our front door for the second time, she was gurgling away happily in my arms. She hated to be put down, had to be carried around or she screamed the roof down. Her tiny little fingers had to be wrapped around someone's thumb or she would screech like a banshee. She must know what abandonment feels like.

"Did you really think they were going to let you keep the baby?" My husband still asks incredulously.

He had stopped objecting to having a baby in the house. From the first time I foisted her onto him while I got her formula ready, she had inveigled her way into his heart and that of our two sons. Each of them now walked into the house with an expectant look and a "Where's Sophia?" The little minx now recognized their voices and shrieked a different shriek in answer to each. My oldest son was "Aaaah," my younger son was "Ba-ba" and my husband was always greeted with a spitty gurgling "Grrrrrr." I was beckoned with a high-pitched wail when she needed food or a change.

Then one day, shortly after we got her adoption papers, they ganged up on me, Grrrrrr, Aaaah and Ba-Ba, with Sophia peeking out from under Ba-Ba's arm.

"Mum, you have to tell us who the mother is," said Aaaah. "Dad said you seem to know her."

"Suppose she comes back for her?" Ba-Ba said, adding fiercely, "We're so *not* giving her back."

"Have you thought of would-be relatives showing up to freeload off us?" Always the banker, my hubby.

I thought they had a right to know. So I told them about Sophia's mother. A maid in a huge mansion several streets away, she was raped by the owner, and when her pregnancy became obvious the owner's wife threatened to have her deported if she didn't leave the country. Her one-way ticket had been booked. I first met her in the library. She was going through midwifery books. We saw one another often and got to meeting regularly once a week at Starbucks. Her English was poor, and she was hesitant to talk about herself. So we talked in general about things. I wondered about her medical care and where she would have the baby. I offered to come with her to the hospital, but she refused. She said she was staying with a friend.

One day, over coffee (she had a smoothie) the baby kicked. She choked on her drink and clutched her stomach.

"He must be a football player," I said, reaching out to caress her stomach as she seemed to be gasping for breath.

"No. Girl." She could barely speak.

"Oh you know that, then?" I smiled. "Girls are a joy."

She shook her head violently. "Not in my country." A haunted look came into her eyes.

"Can I help you in some way?" I tried gently.

No answer.

I slipped my business card into her hand and prepared to leave.

"Call me if you need help. If you are flying 'back home' next week, you must know no airline will allow you in that condition."

Still no answer. She looked beyond tears.

"Be well, child." She looked defenseless. "Look after yourself and the little one."

Finally a tiny smile.

"Wonderful, I know you'll be all right." Funny how we say the most inane things when we are flummoxed by a situation. I hung on to my cheery smile.

"What will you name her?" I asked.

"Sophia."

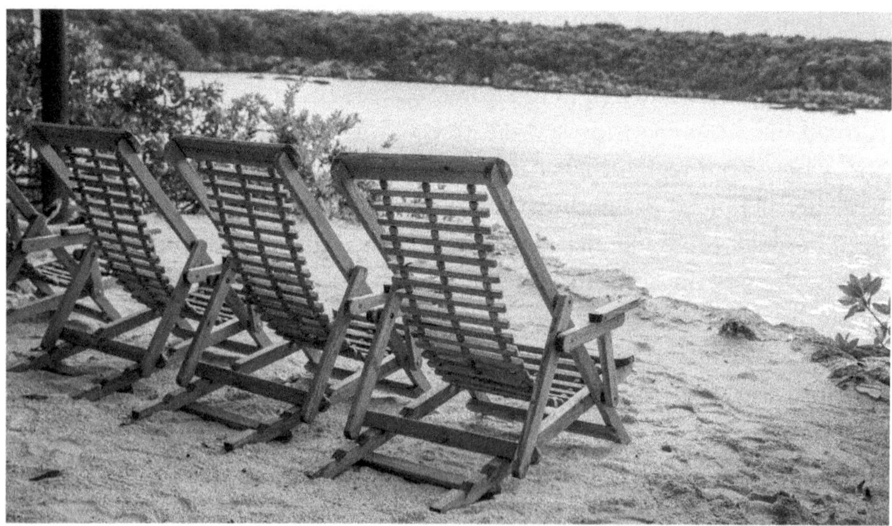

'Take a Moment' by Ash Anthony Xavier

RISE UP! RISE ABOVE!

the journey to a LIFE of POSSIBILITY
begins with such promise
dreams, plans, take flight
the road opens, the UNIVERSE beckons
and then LIFE happens.

out of dark shadows come the denigrators
the stealers of VISION
ANCHORS that dredge the past
dragging bygones into the present
weighting the NOW
TARNISHING the tomorrows
with tainted visions of DIMINISHED glory
LOWERED expectations, shackling HESITANCY
rise ABOVE!

rise above fissures in the road
dug into ever widening CHASMS
by busybody naysayers
whose idea of CREATIVITY
is to create unsurpassable RIFTS
in the pathway of true CREATORS
they purloin and distort the VISION of dreamers
piggybacking to GLORY.
know THEM for WHAT they are
mere potholes, stumbling blocks
to be avoided—circumnavigated
RECLAIM your journey—eyes on the road AHEAD
RISE Up! Rise ABOVE!

Keen to the whisper of the UNIVERSE
to DIVINE intervention
showing YOU that THEY who hurt CALLOUSLY are
UNWORTHY of YOUR headspace
WALK by, walk ON
RISE up! Rise ABOVE!

HOPE on the horizon dimmed by DARK cloud
shelter from the ACID rain
you KNOW the sun is there
it will shine AGAIN another day
WAIT for the clearing

eye on the PRIZE—the prizeS
bucket list wishes splashed on a LIFE MAP
some stick, some don't
what's there is MEANT TO BE. BELIEVE it.
the fallen stars that still SHINE bright
PICK THEM UP, pin them UP, and then
THEN
crawl, limp, RUN, onward and upward
toward your stars, your dreams
your LIFE MAP destinations
rise UP—rise ABOVE.
RISE Up! Rise ABOVE!

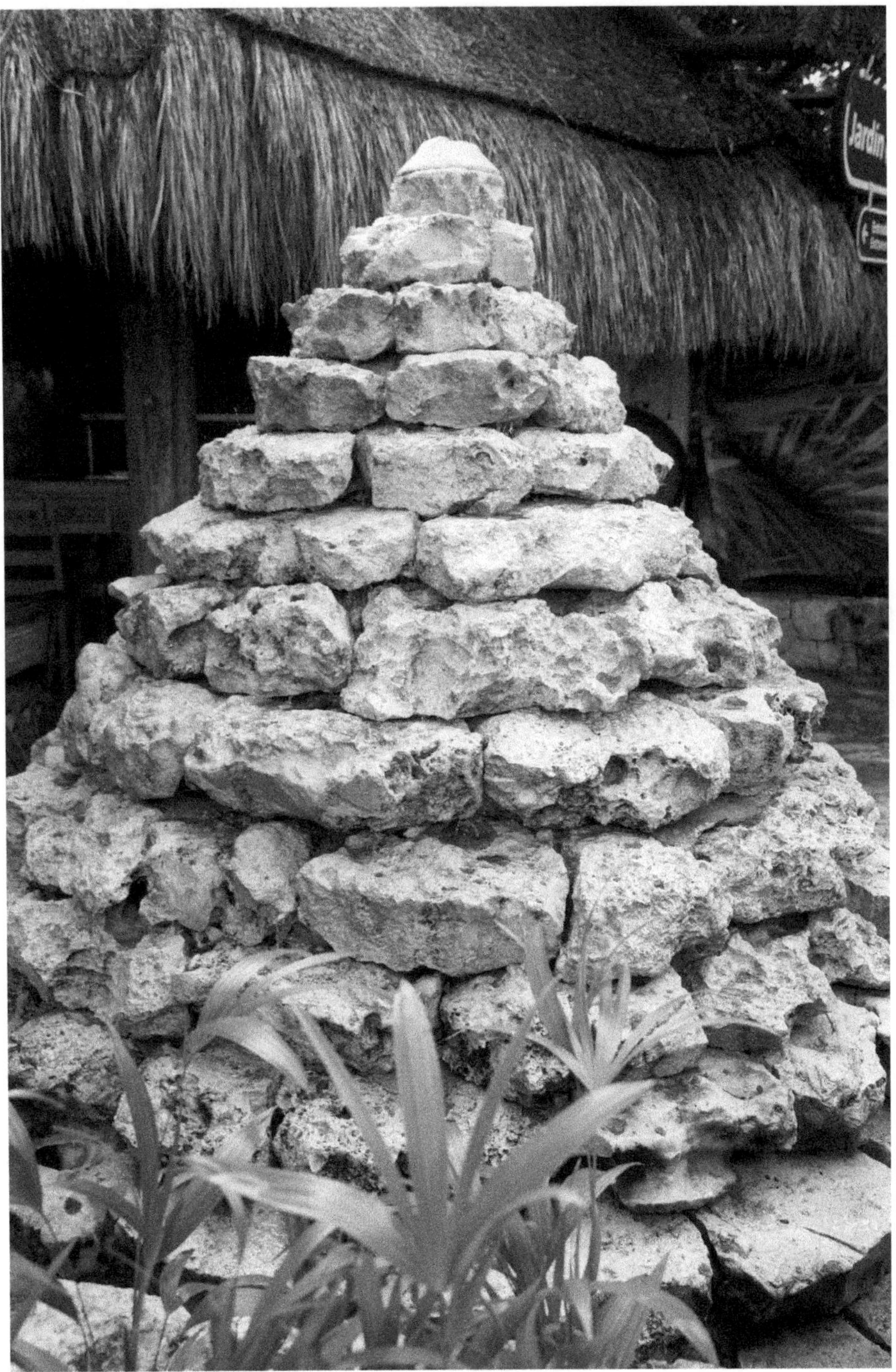

'Symmetry Asymmetry' by Ash Anthony Xavier

TRIBUTE TO CANADA

Against blue skies and darkening horizons
Over vast vistas that trace the earth
From ocean to ocean the banner is raised
Across this magnificent land of ours.
How proud we sing our anthem
Its fine refrain soars from hearts
A symbol of national unity
For the sons and daughters of this land.

A maple leaf emblem now renowned
For values core to our identity
Respect for life and freedom,
Justice and compassion,
A pledge to keep the peace,
At home or on alien soil.
A flag seen as a symbol of hope
A beacon that lights the world.

We who come to these shores
Seeking peace and harmony,
These values pledge to defend forever,
This identity espouse from the heart.
We'll walk in the steps of the forefathers
Wearing the cloak of national pride
With joy we'll join the proud refrain
Paying tribute to Canada!

TOPPLING OF AN IDOL

I came to hear him read
Anticipation seeped through pores
Eager expectation
Ears strained from the back of the room
To catch the first sound
Of that revered presence at the podium.
Over the heads of distraction
I craned to glimpse my idol
Prepared to be transported
Mesmerized
Mindful of every word
Pure gold
Universal
Timeless
Words of a master of words.
His six volumes
Lined the top shelf of my prized collection
Never lent out.
Master writer.

Then he came up
Stooped
Like one defeated
Disillusionment was there
In his eyes, in his voice
Shading the acuity of his vision
The words somehow seemed leaden.
Feeling cheated
I left

HAIKU

Cherry blossom theme

Spring's brushstrokes create
Flourishes of snowy white
Cherry blossom blooms

Cherry blossom blooms
Renew the promise of Spring
Gifts of Hope and Faith

Spring chases winter
Birthing trees of snowy white
Cherry blossom blooms

***Cheryl Antao-Xavier** is an author, editor and publisher. She has published two collections of poetry* Dance of the Peacock, *2008 and* Bruised but Unbroken, *2011. Her first children's book published in English (2014) and French (2015) is entitled* Life in Maple Woods; *the book is the first in a series on the theme of diversity and integration. Her long poem 'RISE Up! Rise ABOVE!' is a rant against bullying in the school and in the workplace.*

John Ambury

CANADA POST BLUES, 2013

'Twas the day before Christmas and all through the mail
Not a Postie was walking, not even a snail
You think you'll be getting your cards at your house?
You better start e-mailing, clicking that mouse.

Letterboxes?—old-fashioned, at least at your door
Take a jaunt to that mass mailbox down by the store
You'll be getting your exercise: "ParticipAction"
And meeting your neighbours, catching up on the action.

So the rates are increasing in wild increments?
They'll make even more money to pay presidents!
Yes, they'll get rid of carriers, that's a sure fact,
But all the *executives'* jobs are intact.

Another small change: they want to charge more
For domestic postal codes not near your door.
We'll be mailing few letters, revenues will decline—
So we'll pay gold for parcels, which we can't ship online.

Get ready to drive to a drug mart location
They've closed down retail at our local post station
You can still pick up packages there, don't be nervous:
From 9 a.m. till noon—now, *there's* some great service!

These changes were all recommended to follow
By outside consultants: not too hard to swallow
Never mind that our own postal corp's CEO
Is on the board of the very same "independent" consulting group
    that made these recommendations TO him—
        so he could recommend to himself
            what he already wanted to do!
                At least, now we know!

It's plain that it's conflict of interest, writ large;
Does Ottawa care? —nah, just pay what they charge!

Well, Chopra, I can't wait to hear your next news—
We can add a new verse to *Canada Post Blues!*

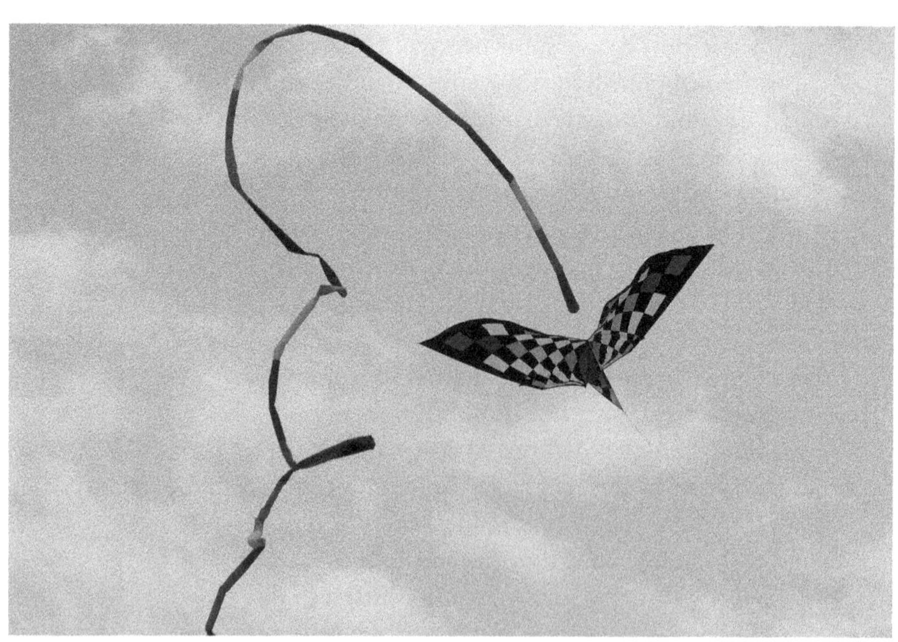

Photograph by Merridy Cox

CIVILIZATION

Fritz Lang is right at home here
Tolkien plays war games in the towers
Orwell watches Big Brother watching
Lewis Carroll fall down the holes.

Only M.C. Escher can find his way around.

But it is not imaginary.
It is Rome and Detroit,
Disneyland and Chichen Itza and Toronto;
It is Jerusalem and Moscow and Babel,
Giza and Las Vegas and Agra.

It is past and to be;
It is then and now:
The once and future world.

It is us, manifest on the planet:
Our chosen dystopia
Our beloved 'civilization.'

(Inspired by the artwork "Market Church at Halle [After Feininger]" by Tsochoy Go.)

HAIKU: WABI SABI SET 1*

Cup
One cup of twenty
a small chip from years of use
this one I treasure.

Rug
Here the dog turned round
to lie down his fourteen years
worn place brings sadness.

Doorway
Hours to paint door frame
but the beauty is scratched on:
ladders of kids' heights.

Car
First dent, she panics
he shrugs; a million grey cars
now ours is unique.

Book
Read once, almost new
but dog-eared at her favourite
erotic passage.

Quilt
New that very week
faint love stain there years later
it still makes them smile.

Beach
No perfect white sand
tourists scorn the gravel shore
we have privacy.

Wedding
Sudden drenching rain
red umbrella saves the day
unforgettable.

Darkroom
Silver halide print
near-invisible tong mark
craftsman's hand revealed.

Contrail
Sunset's ideal glow
marred by curving contrail streak:
art superimposed.

Felicity
Awkward birth defect
she walks with a sideways limp
like all perfect cats.

Primitives
Painter's perception
crude figures, no perspective
art is not drafting.

Love
If you were perfect
I could not match your standard
I love what you are.

** Wabi sabi is, loosely, the oriental philosophy that an object with imperfections (such as those caused by hand-crafting or age and wear) has character, and is more beautiful than one that is flawless.*

ICE STORM

The ice came overnight as freezing rain—
fell wet and froze solid on everything
covered every fencepost and bough and snowdrift
with a thick oppressive coating
broke off big tree-limbs with its weight
took down power lines.
The next morning there was no sun
to make those sparkling-diamond ice photos you see sometimes
just shades of grey: iron and pewter and tarnished silver.

Down by the back fence a dark shape lay
on the hard-crusted snow.
A black squirrel it turned out to be, frozen
never made it to his safe cozy home
high up in a wind-cracking maple:
just an unheated nest of dry leaves and twigs
but warm with his family's body heat.

In bitter cold, the heat was off for a few days
most of the week in some parts of the city
Joanne down the street survived by wearing her mink coat to bed
some of us stayed with family or friends
or huddled in school gyms
but a few died — a few people
with no resources, no options.
Not many, but it made the news.
I didn't know them.

I didn't know the squirrel either
but somehow he was my neighbour, my clan
I shuddered, feeling the desperate freezing of his flesh
ice crystals slowly solidifying his blood after he fell
and mostly, his hopelessness.
His death was the one that touched me most.

ODE TO A FEAR-MONGERING TREE-HUGGER

Suzuki said we'd clear-cut all the hills
We'd have no oxygen to feed our sprawl
But I saw seedlings planted by the mills:
Perhaps Suzuki didn't know it all!
    Yet water, trees and air are getting tight—
    Perhaps Suzuki really had it right?

Suzuki said the tar sands were a mess
And cars' exhaust, the planet's death would bring
But God gave us that oil, our lives to bless:
Perhaps that wise guy didn't know a thing!
    Yet now the earth's condition does appal—
    Perhaps I should have listened, after all?

Suzuki said we'd foul the seas with crap
We'd have no water clean enough to drink
But melting glaciers still fill my tap:
Perhaps the "expert" needs another think!
    Yet now our fragile world begins to croak—
    Perhaps Suzuki knew whereof he spoke?

OVER IT

Over it?
Sure I'm over it
nothing lasts for ever, right?

Over it?
Why not, it was nothing.
Okay, it felt like something at the time—
like you'd grabbed me by the heart
and made me fall like a schoolboy
showed me how Tom Sawyer felt about Becky Thatcher
and why Romeo pined like an idiot under that balcony.
But in the grand scheme of things, it was nothing.

Over it?
Why not, I never needed you.
Even though you were the one who made me feel alive
made me want to keep you warm
made me feel I was strong and had an effect on you
made me feel wanted, needed
like I could give you something nobody else could
like I could get you past the pain
even knowing I could never be him
but not needing to be
because you wanted me for myself.

Over it?
Why not, you never loved me.
Even though you loved how I made you feel
loved that I wanted you for your eyes and your smile and your voice
as well as your body
loved that I waited patiently through your unsure times
loved your own oh-my-God responses,
and the wetness that gave you away
under the influence of those special touches—
loved that I discovered your deepest secret desires
and met them; and loved that you could meet mine too.

Over it?
Sure I'm over it.
I just can't get over you.

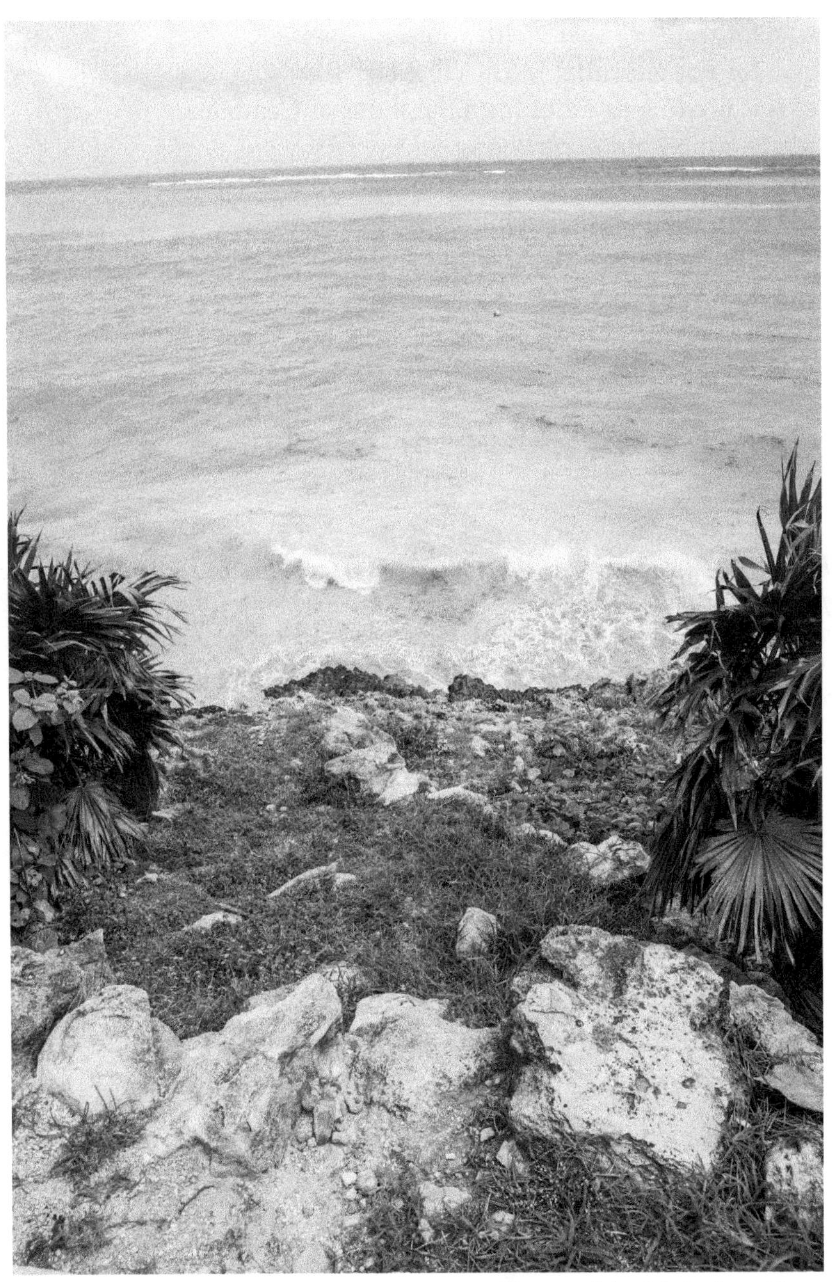

Photograph by Ash Anthony Xavier

THE POETS: B.P.

What pressures you to sing?
    Is it aching for life lost
    for time not spent with your son
    for not returning lovers' clinging?
or is it needing to shout from the slums of Cambodia
what you feel but don't know
what happens when lightning shudders your bones
when emotions ignite your synapses?
    The hauntings that tear you apart
and hold you together
as you lose your breath, yet speak?

(for Brandon Pitts, on his collection Pressure To Sing*)*

John Ambury's *poetry varies widely in both subject matter and style. His work has appeared in* Canadian Voices *(Vols. 1 and 2),* Canadian Imprints *(Vols. 1 and 2),* Verse Afire *and* The Courtneypark Connection 2013. *He has a background in technical writing and editing, and is in demand as a freelance editor, proofreader, and poetry reviewer.*

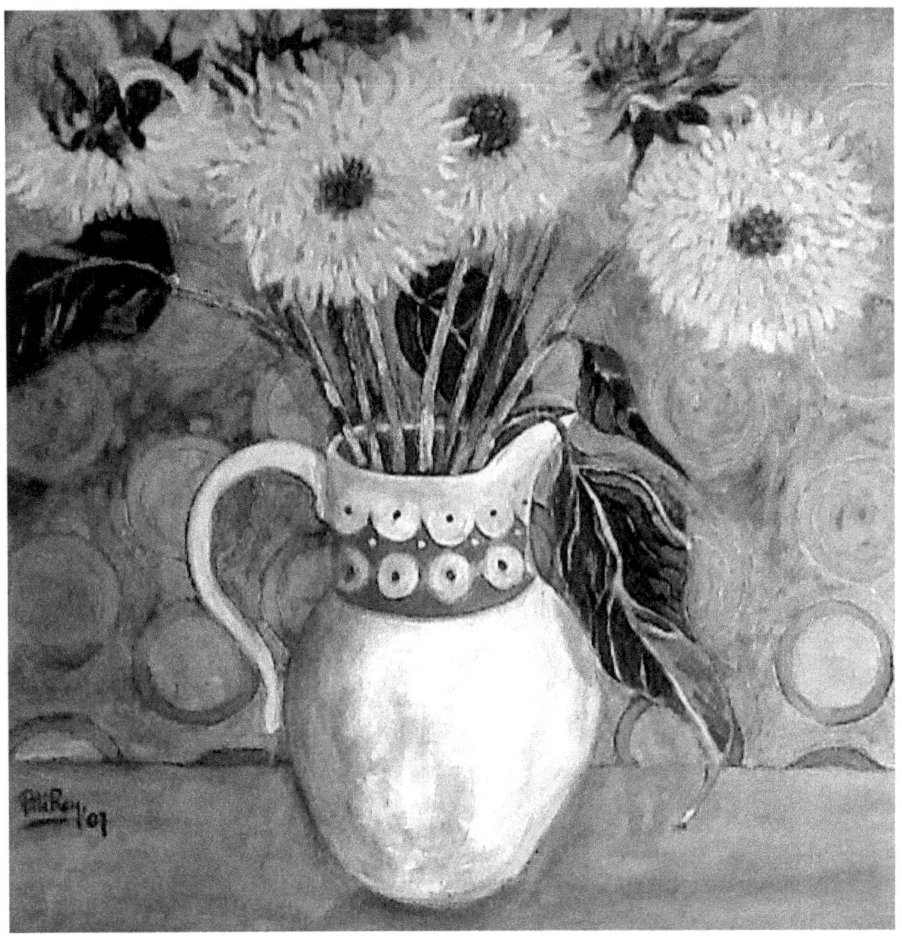

Painting by Pilar Rey de Castro

Nina Munteanu

A SUBTLE MATTER

I gaze out the window of my new apartment and wonder if the trees will ever turn. Or will the leaves just wither, brown and drop to the ground in anonymous heaps?

My mind strays home to Quebec, a landscape where the recurrence of change lies under the sway of cold and drought, blossom and seed. Where the wind is like a fist. I used to watch it snatch the leaves and scatter flaming colours across the road. They soared like flocks of exotic birds, vaulting to a chorus of a chaotic harmony. I'd kick the leaf piles along the roadside and watch the wind beguile the odd leaf to a solo performance.

But I've chosen to pursue my studies here, in Vancouver, BC, where the Olympian conifers defy the seasons and command passive subjugation on an unmoving stage. Here nature has no clock. She stands still. Glancing at my watch, I grab my jacket and head for the university. The old café that I pass every day looks inviting. Longing for coffee, I enter. The dirty windows barely let in enough light to see. I smell lemon wood polish, cooking grease and old furniture. Johnny Lang drawls: "*Lie to me and tell me everything's all right…*" A smile tugs at my lips. This isn't Starbucks.

As I approach the service counter, I glimpse a young bearded man seated at a table. He's wearing the same checkered shirt he wore during registration day when we shared a conversation while waiting in line. Does he remember me? I order a coffee then fumble with the milk and sugar. Carefully balancing the mug, I wander to a table close to his, wanting to share his company but not wanting to impose. He sprawls, reading a ragged paperback held in one hand and stroking his beverage with the other.

As I stand poised at the chair, I catch him looking in my direction with a shy but inviting smile. He puts down the book. When our eyes meet, his smile broadens and he says in a pleasant tenor voice, "Hi."

I smile back, remembering the deep stare of those feral eyes. "Hi." My hand grips the chair back haltingly.

Sensing my indecision, he stutters, "W-would you care to join me?"

"Okay," I respond, feeling my cheeks warm under his guileless gaze. I contrast his awkward invitation to the boisterous charm of Eric, my ex-boyfriend back east, and find this young man's unassuming coyness refreshing.

As I take the seat across from him, he adds, “You’re Sarah, aren’t you?”

“Yes.” I can’t remember his name.

“Jim,” he reminds me. “Come to this hole often?”

“First time,” I admit with a nervous smile.

“Ah, that explains why you ordered the coffee,” he says, leaning back in his chair and scratching his beard.

I notice he’s drinking apple juice and grin. “That bad, eh?” I sip the coffee and sadly agree. Definitely not Starbucks!

“You’re studying to be a botanist, aren’t you?”

I nod, stunned that he remembers my area of specialization. I can’t remember his.

“Maybe you can trace its origin,” he says with a crooked smile, pointing to the coffee. His eyes sparkle with amusement.

“Or maybe just use it in my chemistry class!” I laugh and lean back.

“How do you like Vancouver? Pretty mild, isn’t it.”

I shuffle my feet and lean forward, thinking of the eastern winds. “A little too mild maybe. I’m from Quebec where the seasons blow in and out. Land of the blizzards, you know. Seems like Vancouver only experiences two seasons: wet and wetter.”

I’m relieved that he laughs. It makes his eyes wrinkle and his tanned face look like leather. I notice that the colour of his eyes match his shirt. He’d blend into the forest easily.

“I know what you mean,” he agrees. “I’m from BC’s interior mountains. We get blizzards too. Since moving to the coast I’ve had to look for the seasons too.” His chestnut eyes draw me in. “Here, Mother Nature’s a subtle matter. You need to sniff her out.”

The clock chimes the hour and he looks up. “Oops! I’m late for class.” He stands up. “Nice talking with you, Sarah. Maybe I’ll see you here again.”

“Sure,” I say. “But I think I’ll order a tea next time.”

“Good idea! Bye.”

“Bye.” I watch him dart out with a wave.

As I stroll toward the campus for my first class, an earthy perfume enfolds me in a heady embrace and I stop to take it in. Inhaling deeply I distinguish a chorus of autumn scents from the heavy musk of decaying vegetation to the sharpness of the earth itself. I could grow to like it.

HENRY

"Hey, Kevo," Tim says, looking up as I am about to step out through the front door of the house we share with two other students. He stabs the paper with his finger. "Here's your chance to be cool." I'm their token dweeb, since I haven't dyed my hair, and I'm the only one who drives an old heap. He flings the paper at me and I catch it. I peer down at the ad for a Triumph sports car. It's reasonably priced. I glance at the VW bug parked out front as Tim, slouched on the couch, continues, "Now you can get rid of that hunk of junk, especially since it's giving you grief with that broken clutch, buddy."

"Yeah," Craig agrees, entering from the kitchen. He takes a great mouthful of his sandwich and speaks in a muffled voice, "You can join the cool cats. We know you have enough money. Your mom left you a pile. Instead of fixing that piece of junk, buy the Triumph. We checked it out this aft. It's sweet!"

I glance at the picture of the Triumph. It's tempting. Then I catch a glimpse of my old car out front through the window. Tim follows my glance. He reads my hesitation and exhales in exasperation. "Geez, Kev, what's with you and that car anyway? What's so special about it? It's all beat up. Your mom smacked it so many times already before you got the car from her."

I inherited the yellow beetle when she died five years ago. There was something about her and old beat up cars. Like Henry. . . .

❧❧

I can still hear my mother defending herself, as she swerved the car into the left lane to the blast of a horn behind us, "But we're just now getting really comfortable with each other, with our creaky joints, what makes us cranky and what makes us hum." She hugged the steering wheel and rocked it like a baby. "How can I abandon Henry now?" She then patted the dash like it was a living being.

"But, Mom," I sank back in my vinyl seat and smelled plastic and gasoline. The car creaked as she slowed at a red light. "Henry's almost dead—"

"Hardly!" She waved her arm and slammed the accelerator. The car sped out of the intersection and wove through traffic, cutting off a Beemer. I cringed as I glimpsed the mad driver waving his arm at us. "This car has lots of spunk left in him, Kevin."

I was nine years old and madly hoping my mom would trade in this tired old Toyota Tercel for the brand new VW Bug she had her eye on. I had visions of sitting in the plush back seat that didn't stick to me during the summer or smell like old runners. I imagined a quiet drive uninterrupted by the car's rude digestive sounds.

As I watched her drive with one hand draped over the wheel and the other poised loosely over the stick shift, I wondered why she clung to this rusty heap. After the mechanic threw his arms in the air and refused to work on the car, Mom still didn't get rid of it. That's when she named it Henry and started talking to it whenever it misbehaved, like the time it stalled in the middle of Patulla Bridge or made loud grinding noises and shimmied when it squealed around a corner.

I still remember the day she drove my best friend and me home from the IMAX movie, Cirque du Soleil's *Journey of Man.* Stroking the dash of the car, she said, "Henry, how about doing a little dance for these boys." We shrieked as the car wiggled down the road to a tune she belted out slightly off key.

I finally asked Mom why she named the car Henry.

"Well, Kevin," she replied with a gleam in her eye, which could have meant a number of things. But I think it meant that she was delighted that I'd asked her. "He's named after a stray cat I knew. I called him Henry, too. He was an ugly, old, white and gray cat, who'd seen a lot of fights. His face and ears were all torn up. And he had an all-grey tail that looked like it'd been stuck on to the rest of his white body as an afterthought. When my cat, Baker, came into heat, Henry courted her." My mom paused and smiled. Her eyes fixed on the distance for a moment, obviously stirred by fond memories. "Henry won her over two younger and larger toms. When she was spayed, he remained her friend. Wild as ever, he came every day and sat with her for a while on our patio. When I moved out of Richmond, I couldn't take him along. It still makes me a little sad that I left him behind. I think Baker missed him too. Now she's dead." My mom looked sad then and I noticed all her wrinkles and the grey hairs in her wild mat of brown hair.

"But, Mom, what does that have to do with this car?" I asked.

"Absolutely nothing," she shrugged. Then she tilted her head and looked pensive again. Her mouth curled into a half smile. "Except they're both old and ugly as sin."

Despite my mom's valiant efforts, Henry the car perished a few years later. He just refused to start one frosty December morning. My uncle, who was a handyman, took a look under the hood. Mom peered from the side, wringing her hands together. Uncle Mat shook his head and informed her that the motor had seized. "Time to get a new car," he said and winked at me. My mom wept as the tow truck pulled Henry away to the scrap yard.

Then she bought a VW Bug. It wasn't new, but it was yellow and it smelled nice inside. The seats were cloth and the car didn't howl around corners. We tried to name it. I came up with Babe, Peewee, and Zeppo. But none of the names stuck.

"The best things are earned, including names," she said. Then she turned to me with a smile and added, "Don't worry, honey. The right name will come to you when you know each other better."

She'd only had the car a few years when she got sick and stopped driving. That's when I got my learner's permit. I practiced lots, taking my mom to and from the hospital and to my uncle's house, where I stayed while Mom was having her treatments.

&

"I'll think about it," I say to Tim and Craig, folding the paper in my hand, and leave the house. As I step into the VW Bug, turn the ignition key and gently press the accelerator, I realize that Mom never did name this car. I toss the newspaper into the back seat and listen to the car creak as I ease it onto the street and my memory conjures the emerald twinkle of her eyes. I find myself saying, "I heard that, Benny," and reach my free hand forward to pat the dash.

Nina Munteanu *is a Canadian ecologist and internationally published novelist of science fiction and fantasy. In addition to eight published novels, Nina has written award-nominated short stories, articles and non-fiction books, which have been translated into several languages throughout the world. Recognition for her work includes the Midwest Book Review Reader's Choice Award, finalist for* Foreword Magazine*'s Book of the Year Award, the SLF Fountain Award, and* The Delta Optimist *Reviewers' Choice. Her collection of short stories on humanity's evolution* Natural Selection *was published by Pixl Press in 2013. The latest in her science fiction thriller trilogy* The Splintered Universe *was published by Starfire in 2014.*

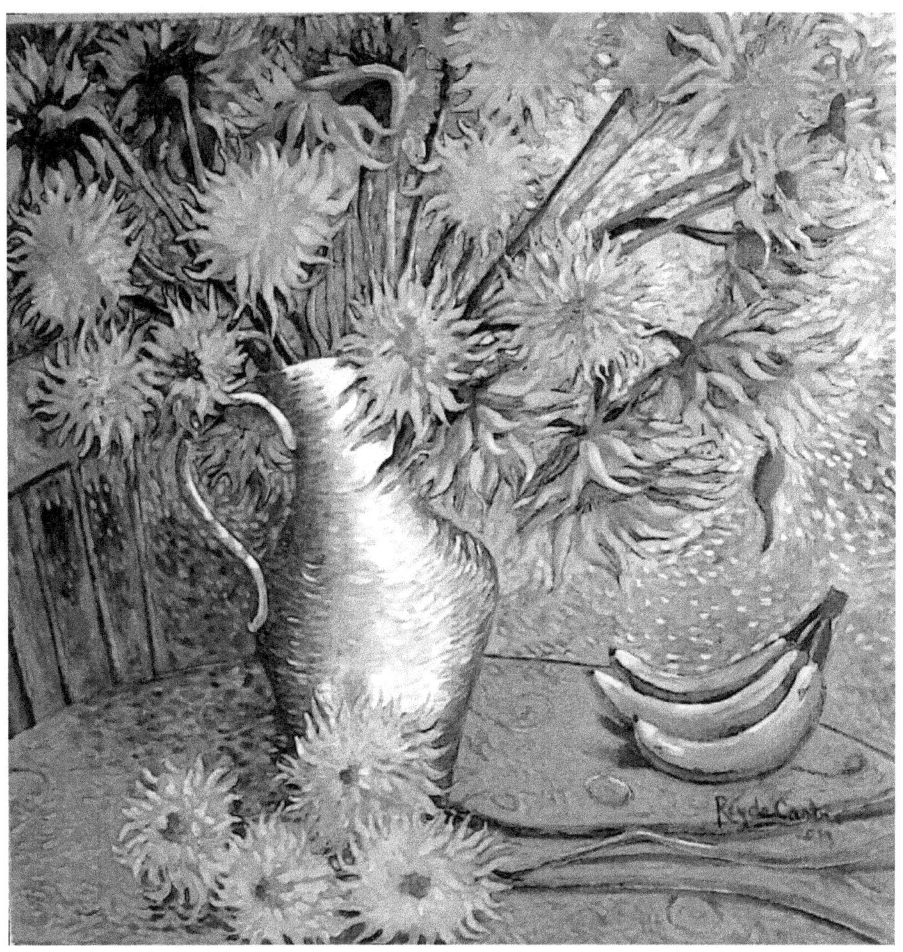

Painting by Pilar Rey de Castro

Lindsay W. Albert

MEMORIES IN STORAGE

No money to keep this rented space
holding boxes filled with my yesterdays
Inevitable is the task before me
to pare down these mountains of boxes
to what will fit in my smaller abode

Out of one box a pair of riding boots
with straw still stuck to the heel
from decades ago as a teenager
living extremes of joy and fear

Box after box after box after box
drowning in a flood of memories
Overwhelmed, exhausted, feeling empty
I step outside for a break

Across the street I see a pear tree in blossom
with branches empty of last year's fruit
A must to allow this year's crop to thrive
Refreshed with clarity I go back inside

My possessions I can now let go of
Item and memory previously perceived as one
now viewed as the separate entities they are
Experiences and memories are with me always
living in storage inside of my mind

MY UN-DER CAT

(In Loving Memory of Marcie)

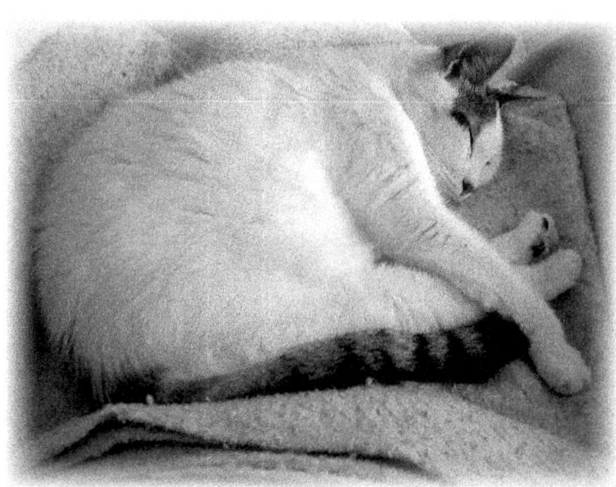

UN-wanted
　　wandering alone on the street
UN-believable
　　how emaciated you were
UN-limited
　　your hope and will to survive
UN-explained
　　how you came to be at my back door
UN-usual
　　your heart-shaped marking
UN-harmed
　　falling eleven stories without a fracture
UN-ending
　　your enthusiasm for life
UN-erring
　　how we saw each other
UN-wavering
　　the devotion shared with each other
UN-dying
　　how I wish your physical life here could be
UN-bearable
　　is my life without you
UN-forgettable
　　memories held of our time together
UN-breakable
　　the loving bond that joins us
UN-conditional
　　what you taught me love could be

H.O.P.E.

Heed
Opposites
Pairs
Emulsify

Honouring
Obstacles
Promotes
Experience

Hardships in life are a present
Opportunities from which to grow
Prompts exploration from within
Evolves a self not known before

Harrowing events are seeds
Offered so we may unearth
Potential lying dormant within us
Exposing new wonders of self

GRIEF IN AN EGGSHELL

Loss begets pain that impels me
to seek refuge inside a shell
A shielding wall to surround me
to keep loss and its pain outside

To my dismay I discover my grief
resides with me inside this shell
From its confines I must break free
or grief smothers me from within

Just as a hatchling who must strive
to break free of its shell to live
not at once, with small cracks and chips
until it emerges safe beyond the shell

Its shell that once was protective
a safe place to begin to grow
no longer provides what's needed
Now to thrive—outside the shell it must go

Resting at times, it draws on new strength
persevering until it breaks free
No going back to life as it was
a different life has now come to be

From my loss is born a new life
fostering strength not known before
In time and when I am ready
beyond the shell I'll venture forth

BORN TO FLY

(Dedicated to Leslie Balmer)

I came to you with a broken wing
My world was spun around
I was stranded upon the ground

With gentle caring and wisdom
never uttering harsh judgmental words
You offered understanding and compassion

You provided a safe haven
where the pain that was trapped inside
could spill out and be put in its place

Healing came from the inside out
New strength was found within
I yearned to soar and to be free

I drew upon newfound courage
to follow where I looked to the sky
Nothing now to hold me back

You patiently walked alongside me
for miles and miles on this healing path
Our work together has triumphed

My wings are strong as they catch the breeze
Riding the wind, climbing to new heights
I am soaring and I am free

LOOK AT ME

(Lessons from a child)

Look at me—what do you see?
Join me in a laughing spree

Look at me—in a pose so cute
Now hand over my arrowroot

Look at me—getting mad
Put the camera down please, Dad

Look at me—with a pensive stare
Who's that holding my teddy bear?

Look at me—what I show is real
My feelings aren't something to conceal

Look at me—I laugh, cry and grin
no holding back the feelings within

Look at me—being my authentic self
not like adults, feelings on the shelf

Look at me—and what you'll learn
It's your inner child whom you yearn

Look at me—now look inside
Let your inner child be your guide

Look at me—I'll show you the way
to learn to play before you go grey

Look at me—living real without concern
Too late for truth once you're in an urn

Look at me—this is your last chance
Being your true self isn't happenstance

RUNAWAY TRAIN

Here I sit on a runaway train
going to I don't know where
Landscape becoming a blur
travelling the rails at breakneck speed
piercing through air like a bullet

I attempt to escape to no avail
The open window steals my breath away
With rhythmic pounding of
wheels joined with the track
deafens me to all other sounds

Freely I chose to come aboard
I'm trapped within its metal grip
To exit now would mean certain death
With every tunnel entry brings
a wave of darkness void of known existence

Light once yearned is hoped to never return
There's only one way to stop this ride of terror
that's to derail the train from upon its track
Send it soaring into the mountainside
to crash and burn until only ashes are left

SEARCHING FOR CALM

Seeking relief from the torment
one way I know all too well
will quickly cease the pain
at least for a little while

The end justifies the means yet
would simultaneously undo
the healing achieved thus far
The cycle of distress repeats

Still a comfort to know
a simple stroke of the blade
carving through flesh to bleed
guarantees to bring relief
by watching pain flow away
on the glistening crimson stream

Though some may think
to die is what's sought
No, it's truly about survival
As blood departs each wound
I'm in control of pain
not pain controlling me
From drifting into numbness
now I can feel again

Time to stop this cycle and
seek a healthier way to cope
to discover a serenity within
as peaceful as a young child snuggled
in the depths of a favourite blanket

ROOM OF DARKNESS

A darkness deep
does fill the room
shadows loom around her

Haunting, taunting
forever there
No peace
is to be found

Four walls
a ceiling and a floor
no door, no windows
no place for light or sun
no way to enter
no way to exit

Confined among dark shadows
unable to discern
who is friend or foe
for they are as one

Against the corner
she huddles alone
her safety counts on this
without motion
or making of a sound
may her location
not be found

TOUCHED BY A WAVE

A rolling wave cresting gently
upon the shore
encompassing the rocks
softly shuffling them
rearranging their space
all too soon
is drawn back
out to sea

Lindsay W. Albert *An avid reader since her preschool days, Lindsay W. Albert (pen name) began writing at 7 years old as a source of healing expression during difficult life experiences. She shares her poetry to impart hope, comfort and healing to her audience as they face their own life challenges. Lindsay's poems have been published in two anthologies:* The Courtneypark Connection 2013 *and* Labour of Love (*Volume 38, December 2013*). *She was a finalist in the Oakville Literary Café Poetry contest (April 2014).*

WE THE EDITORS…

…thank the contributors to *The Literary Connection Volume I* for sharing their creative work and inspiration. It was a pleasure putting this anthology together. We hope you are as proud of this publication as we are. We wish you success in your writing. Here's a bit about us…

Cheryl Antao-Xavier has a degree in English Literature and studied writing, editing and publishing at Ryerson. She has over twenty years' experience in various aspects of publishing from writing, editing, design to print/e-publishing. Combining these skills and a passion for the written word, she set up In Our Words Inc. in 2008 to publish and promote Canadian writing. To date, IOWI has published over 50 titles. She is also an editor on the literary website chapterandverse.ca. Most often you'll find her firmly—and blissfully—rooted in her home office oasis in Streetsville, Ontario.

Nina Munteanu is an award-winning novelist, essayist and short story author. She co-edits Europa SF and serves as professional editor for Grimoire Books (USA) and Future Fiction (Italy). Nina also teaches writing at the University of Toronto and George Brown College. She regularly speaks at writing conferences and conventions in Canada and has been coaching writers to publication for over fifteen years. Her writing guidebooks are used in colleges and universities throughout North America and in Europe. She travels a lot for work and pleasure, but is most often in the Greater Toronto Area.

Merridy Cox Bradley is a freelance technical writer and editor with experience in thesaurus-building and other such three-dimensional cross-paragraph puzzles. Her background is in biology (B.Sc.) and museums (M.Msl.), and she has a love of the English language. She is completing an English manual with excerpts and photographs in a blog entitled www.englishmanual.wordpress.com. Her published work, as an editor, includes e-book *Edwardian Annotated Pets and How to Keep Them, Part I: Beasts.* You may find her in Toronto, Mississauga, Peterborough, or occasionally Ottawa, Ontario, Canada.

Saima S. Hussain was commissioned to research and write a book about the contributions that were made by Arabs in the fields of medicine, astronomy, arts, education, etc. *The Arab World Thought of It: Inventions, Innovations and Amazing Facts* (Annick Press, Toronto) was published in 2013. That same year, the book won a Best Book award from the Carolina Center for the Study of the Middle East and Muslim Civilization. In 2014, it received an honourable mention at the Arab American Book Awards (Arab American National Museum) in the Children/Young Adult category.

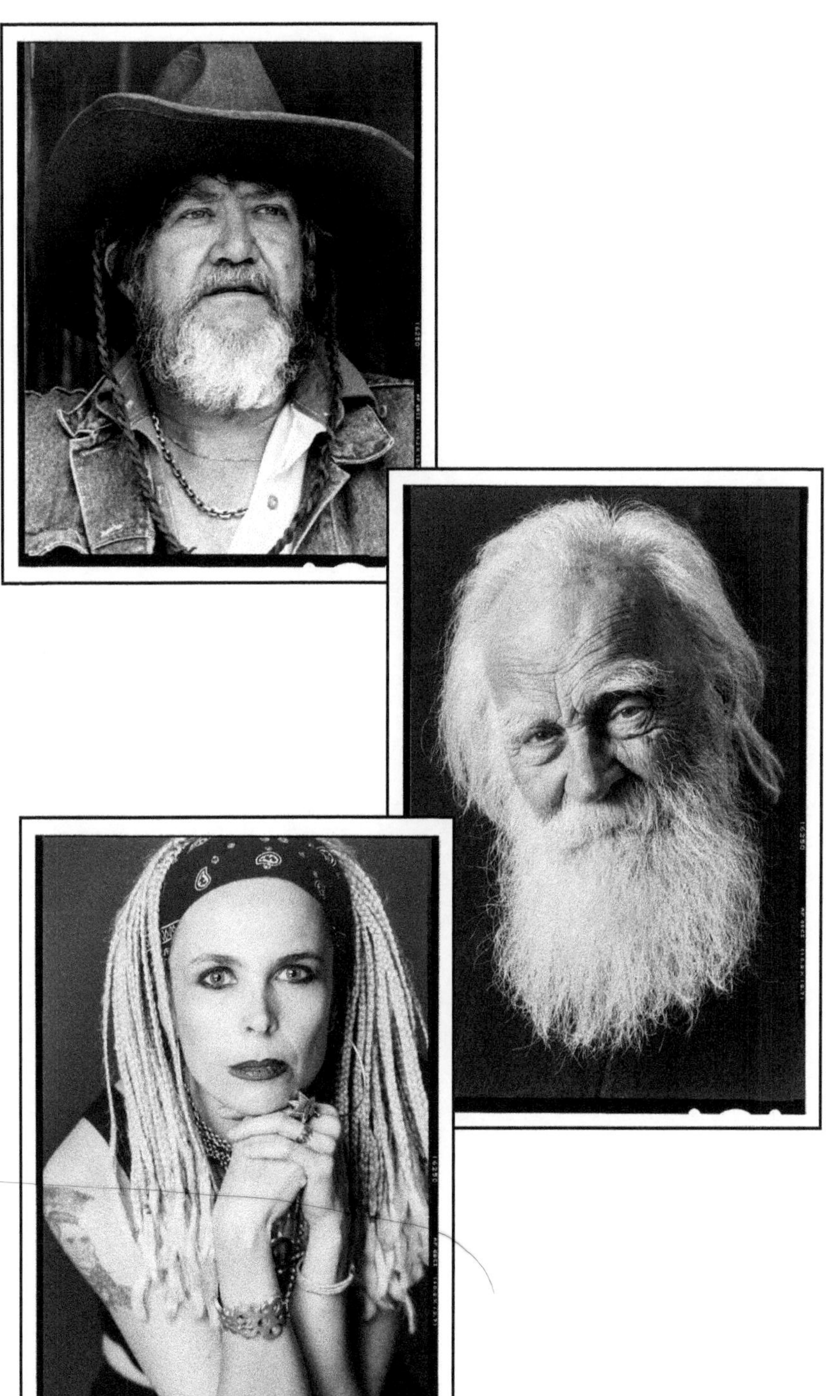

Portraits by Lisa Mininni

www.ingramcontent.com/pod-product-compliance
Ingram Content Group UK Ltd.
Pitfield, Milton Keynes, MK11 3LW, UK
UKHW020142250726
13967UKWH00002B/805